# LEARNING
# THE ROPES

# LEARNING THE ROPES

---

*The Insider's Guide to*
*Winning at Work*

Robin,
Continued Success
to you!
Camille Primm
10/07

# Camille M. Primm

**To order additional copies of this book, contact:**
Xlibris Corporation
1-888-795-4274
www.Xlibris.com
Orders@Xlibris.com
19758

# CONTENTS

## Chapter Four
## Attitude — It's Your Choice

## Chapter Five
## Communicating to Get What You Want

## Chapter Six
## Work Place Cultures

# Chapter Seven
## Skills that Spell "S-E-C-U-R-I-T-Y"

# Chapter Eight
## Work Place Politics, Relationships and Schmoozing

# Chapter Nine
## Shamelessly Marketing Your Talents

## Chapter Ten
## Leading the Pack — Management Success Skills

## Dedication

To
Helen Catherine and Jules Richard Primm
My Extraordinary Parents

From Them I Have Learned That Life Is an Adventure
Where the Only Limitations Are Self-Imposed

# Acknowledgements

So many people have encouraged my writing efforts; it is difficult to recognize them all individually. The contents of this book represent my experiences in life and work, thus anyone involved in those experiences is a contributor. My deepest appreciation goes out to all who have contributed to my learning and growth, supported me during my failures, and helped to celebrate my successes.

## Credits

Copy Editor — Angela Davis
Cover Design — Julia Kroge
Cover Photo — Randy Rovang, www.yourpix.com

# Forward

In 1991, I experienced one of the most significant rites of passage of the American Worker. I was laid off. This event started a chain reaction opening a whole new world for me. While this episode in my life was emotionally charged, it changed me in ways that I could never have predicted.

I created a whole new chapter in my professional life by pulling together my 20 years of work experience. The portfolio career I hatched is a combination of my passions, skills, natural talents, personality traits, and ideal work style.

I am not going to lie and say it has been easy, but one thing I know for sure is that the rocky paths are the ones that lead to the most wondrous vistas. If I had remained in my original career as a tenured teacher, I would be eligible for full retirement. Instead, the path I carved out will most likely lead to never really retiring—I am having too much fun! The trade-off has been a work life rich with experiences, trials and tribulations, and successes that could fill a book. So here it is!

# Introduction

The shifts in the world of work were so dramatic during the 1990's that many workers are now confused and frustrated. Baby Boomers were programmed to select a career path, complete the training necessary for success, put their noses to the grindstone, and carry on for the next 40+ years.

After experiencing a life changing layoff in 1991, I opted to create a portfolio career by pulling together the pieces of my prior work experience that I most enjoyed. This choice led to coaching individuals who had been downsized, right-sized, pink-slipped, de-installed, fired, outsourced, laid off, reengineered, or reorganized. In other words, working with people whose world was turned upside down due to job loss.

I observed that many experienced a loss of self-esteem, a declining sense of security, frustration, and nearly always at the top of the list . . . a sense of betrayal. The lesson learned was that no matter how much extra work one did, no matter how many hours one put in on weekends and evenings, no one is exempt from the risk of a layoff. The rules have changed so dramatically that workers are at a loss for what to do. How can they get ahead when a new boss rotates in every few months? When the company eliminates their jobs every couple of years? When seniority doesn't mean security?

I frequently hear the complaint that employees have "no control" over their situation. This is where I encourage you to embrace a different thought process. In times of ambiguity, you must be crystal clear about where YOU want to end up. You must put your own goals in the forefront, or you will no doubt be a "worker bee" supporting others in realizing their goals.

The biggest differentiator in the success of the job seeker is knowing the ropes. The keys to moving forward are:

**Resilience, Optimism, Productivity, Education, and Skills.**

When transitioning to a new workplace, employees are often unsure about the rules and how to get things done. Mergers cause huge culture shifts, and company politics can be baffling. When we stayed in a job for life, we knew the players, how things worked, how to survive, and what our place was. Now that we change jobs every 2-5 years, we have to be flexible and adapt to new systems and environments on a continuing basis.

If all the changes in your work environment have left you at a loss about how to act and react, you will find the answers in *Learning the Ropes*. If you are just embarking on your career path, you can ease and accelerate your learning curve by referring to these pages. In short, *Learning the Ropes* is the guidebook for *all workers* and will support *your* success!

This book breaks down the key areas on which to focus in order to help you succeed and thrive in any work environment. To rise as high as you want to rise. To deal with any work situation diplomatically, gracefully, and professionally. Use it to guide you through the ever-changing world of work; you will see your stress level diminish and your success level multiply!

# About the Author

Camille M. Primm, is a career strategist, speaker, and writer with a successful track record in facilitating seminars and consulting with organizations nationwide. Through her firm, PrimmTime Communications, she has worked with employees of varied industries including: utilities, manufacturing, health care, aerospace, high tech, pharmaceuticals, tobacco, banking, government, insurance and universities.

An accomplished leader, Camille is known for her interactive motivational style and use of humor to underscore key points. She personifies the concepts of change management, career fitness, and leadership development. Her finely tuned communication skills enable her to relate to audiences of all sizes and cultures.

Camille is a dynamic speaker. Having made hundreds of presentations to corporate audiences, her topics have included thriving in a changing environment, strategic career management, leadership development, employee retention, controlling stress and thinking optimistically.

A proponent of interest-driven careers, Camille is a change agent with a broad base of business expertise. Her career path includes education, project management, international business, coaching, writing, consulting, and operating her training firm.

In 1991, Camille turned her long-time interest in career development to the world of outplacement and career development. She has managed huge reorganization projects and facilitated hundreds of career transition seminars. As a coach, Camille has partnered with over 2,500 professionals in identifying and reaching their career goals.

Several years ago, Camille's work began to gain international recognition via career Internet sites. Over 100 of her articles have been published and have guided thousands of workers through transitions. In addition, ten Internet streaming video clips showcase Camille's advice and offer employees at all stages of their careers distilled tips for succeeding at work.

Camille holds a BA in Education and German with a minor in public speaking, and is a Longwood University alumna. She resides in San Diego, CA.

# History of Author's Paid Jobs

To put the Author's views into perspective, following is a list of her paid positions to date. Perhaps it will inspire you to build your own "interest-driven" career and to do whatever it takes to pursue your own dreams.

| Job Title | Place |
| --- | --- |
| 1. Killing Flies for The City | Mobile, AL |
| 2. Lemonade Stand | Albuquerque, NM |
| 3. Baby Sitter | CA, VA, France, Germany |
| 4. Part-Time Nanny | Alexandria, VA |
| 5. Dressing Room Clerk | Patch Barracks PX, Stuttgart, Germany |
| 6. Dry Cleaner/Laundry Counter Clerk | Patch Barracks PX, Stuttgart, Germany |
| 7. Waitress | Longwood University, VA |
| 8. Newspaper Route | Longwood University, VA |
| 9. Office Manager | Enlisted Club - Naval Supply Center, Charleston, SC |
| 10. Bartender | Richmond, VA |
| 11. German Teacher | Oakton HS, Alexandria, VA |
| 12. Sales Clerk | DeYoung Shoes, Alexandria, VA |
| 13. Sales Clerk | Leggett's, Manassas, VA |
| 14. International Tour Guide | Alexandria, VA |
| 15. German Teacher/Speech Teacher/Department Chairman | Groveton HS, Alexandria, VA |
| 16. German Club/German Honor Society/Keyette Club Sponsor | Groveton HS, Alexandria, VA |
| 17. Intramural Sponsor | Groveton HS, Alexandria, VA |
| 18. Map Reader – Calculator | City of Alexandria, VA |
| 19. Office Assistant | Piedmont Airlines, Washington, DC |
| 20. Waitress | The Clipper, Alexandria, VA |
| 21. Waitress | The Zephyr Room, Washington, DC |
| 22. Waitress | Ireland's Own, Alexandria, VA |
| 23. German Language Tutor | Alexandria, VA |
| 24. Waitress | Das Rad, Sindelfingen, Germany |
| 25. Co-Owner/Manager | Oberhaus Cafe, Boeblingen, Germany |
| 26. Sales Associate | Barter Associates, Charlotte, NC |
| 27. Sales Associate | TMC Communications, Charlotte, NC |
| 28. Supervisor/Director | Charlotte Foreign Trade Zone, NC |
| 29. Importer/Distributor | Charlotte, NC |
| 30. President | Global Technology Center, Charlotte, NC |

| 31. Freelance Consultant | Charlotte Convention Center, NC |
| 32. Consultant/Trainer/Project Manager | Drake Beam Morin, Charlotte, NC |
| 33. Consultant/Trainer/Project Manager | Lee Hecht Harrison, San Diego, CA |
| 34. Psychic Friend | Psychic Hotline, San Diego, CA |
| 35. Telelcommunications Researcher | Equifax, San Diego CA |
| 36. Market Researcher | Luth Research, San Diego CA |
| 37. Consultant | PrimmTime Communications, San Digeo, CA |
| 38. Speaker | PrimmTime Communications, San Digeo, CA |
| 39. Writer | kforce.com, Tampa, FL |
| 40. Video Subject Matter Expert/Actor | kforce.com, Tampa, FL |
| 41. Corporate Trainer/Facilitator | PrimmTime Communications, San Digeo, CA |
| 42. Executive Coach | PrimmTime Communications, San Digeo, CA |
| 43. Author | PrimmTime Communications, San Digeo, CA |

# CHAPTER ONE

## Change is Constant . . . Learn to Love It!

# The Change Game

---

*"Those who refuse to change are beautifully
prepared to live in a world
that no longer exists."*

— *Eric Hoffer*

---

W hen we stop changing, we stop growing. Intellectually, most of us have accepted that without change, we will eventually become extinct. So why do we exert so much energy to *avoid* change?

Many people look at change as an end, rather than a process. The feelings of being out of control and unable to make the choices that often accompany change is an uncomfortable one. The key is to remember *we always have choices and we are always in control.*

In times of ambiguity, it is imperative that you get *crystal clear* on what *you* want. If you are not heading in the direction of your own goals, you are just another worker bee helping someone else reach *their* goals.

Here are a few strategies to be on top of your own change game.

## Over-Communicate

When a lot of changes are occurring, our imaginations run

wild. We speculate. And, while there do appear to be some gifted psychics out there, our imagination is often worse than the real thing. Over-communicating these thoughts can help you deal with your fears. Some tips include:

- Talk about the changes you are experiencing with someone you trust.
- Ask for information.
- Let others know what you are thinking.
- Discuss your fears with a friend or loved one.
- Lay the groundwork for future actions.
- Deal with the facts you must face.

## Brainstorm About Solutions

Creativity is a skill that can be developed. When faced with a change, get out your paper and pen and start writing. Forget about reality—just list at least 20 possible ways of handling the change. When you let your ideas flow, it primes the pump for more ideas. Keep your lists in file folders and refer to them often when making changes and decisions for possible actions.

## Know What Makes You Tick

The idea of a perfect alignment in our work is simple, yet often overlooked. We all have skills that are stale, values that have changed over the years and are motivated by various factors such as money, freedom, power or challenge. Take time out to assess your personality traits, life and work values, key skills and the work environment in which you feel most comfortable. When you live and work in alignment with your values, there are fewer roadblocks to higher levels of success.

## Be Aware of Trends

Being current with what is happening in your industry,

and the world at large, is one of the most empowering ways to proactively manage change. There are so-called "experts" out there who, if they read one current book, would realize they were totally outdated. When you are aware of trends, and change with them, you will see the coming patterns and be on *top* of the wave, instead of having it crash down on you.

## Your Circle of Influence Includes Yourself

Proactive people focus their attention and energy on things they actually have influence over. This results in their ability to control the outcome of their efforts and increases the chances of getting what they want. It is so obvious that many of us tend to overlook it. The bulk of what we worry about never happens. When we take that same amount of energy and use it to deal with what actually *does* happen, we can be amazed at our ability to make wise choices. In reality, we have much more control than we realize . . . or are willing to take!

## Tune in to Your Internal Voices

What messages are your internal tapes playing day in and day out? On your way to a meeting, is your tape listing all of the things that might go wrong, or are you focusing on the positive things that may occur? The subconscious knows no difference between fact and fiction. Pay attention to your internal voices. Are they filling you with negatives or positives? Once you are aware of these messages and the power of them, eject the negatives and tape over them with positive messages that bring you closer to your goals.

## Identify the Actions You Will Take to Thrive

The change model of Awareness, Acceptance, Action is a

powerful one. Once you are fully conscious of the changes going on around you, decide what you are going to *do* about them. Taking charge is the key to getting what you want . . . and deserve. By creating Plans A, B and C, you decide how you will react to situations and use them to reach your own goals. Remember that there are many means to an end. If your first plan doesn't fall into place, switch over to the second one. By using this strategy, you will never be a "victim" who whines about the things that *happen* to them. You will be a person who makes intelligent choices on how you *react* to events around you.

## Take a Break

In our fast-paced world, we often are so task and goal-oriented, we forget the fact that "thinking" is part of the process. Why not call in "well" today and spend a few hours doing something that will allow you to just *exist*. Something as simple as going to the park and changing your scenery might be the key that opens your greatest thoughts. Some of the most powerful ideas pop into our minds *when we have made some room*.

Human existence is all about change—a wonderful vehicle for growth. Your ability to control your life rests in the choices you make. Chose to react to change with intelligence, patience and clarity. It's your life—choose wisely!

# Coping With Change At Work

*"Are you a thermometer or a thermostat? A
thermometer only reflects
the temperature of its environment, adjusting
to the situation. But a thermostat initiates
action to change the temperature
in its environment."*

— Nido Qubein

"The only constant is change." Sound familiar? Well, the Greek philosopher Heraclitus made this comment some 2,500 years ago. And we think we have it bad—at least today we have technology tools to help us keep up with the dizzying rate of daily shifts in our lives.

The tendency of intelligent beings is to resist change with all the energy we can muster. We protest and push and pull and find that we are not only tired, but we *still* do not get our way! This leads to more frustration and resentment, and eventually a feeling that we have no control over our lives and careers.

Think back to a song we all learned in grade school— "Row, Row, Row Your Boat". Remember singing that one happily with your classmates? When things get tough, bring that little song back into your mind. It says "Row your boat"—not anyone else's. So, concentrate on what you can control regarding your personal work situation. What is everyone else doing? What is the company doing? Forget about it! Conserve your energy and use it to better your own situation.

The next line of the tune says "Gently *down* the stream". It doesn't say to row *up* the stream—so if you relax and go with the flow, you won't get worn out resisting the current. If you don't like the tide of things in your current work, focus on the items that you actually can impact. After all, you are *not* going to be able to single-handedly change the direction of the entire company—right?

"Merrily, Merrily, Merrily, Merrily—life is but a *dream*." If you keep that little phrase at the forefront of your plans, you will remember that we are allowed to have fun—and we are supposed to be doing the type of work that we love and dream about.

Here are a few ways you can make the advice from this song work for your career.

- First, remember that change is a process—not an event. For instance, if your job is eliminated, the change isn't over the day you empty out your desk. It is a process lasting weeks—maybe even months. There is a lot to learn. What key skills do you want to market? Are you willing to relocate? How will you research target companies? How will you position the layoff situation when you run into friends? The adjustment from the layoff involves many details. If you understand this concept and look at it from that perspective, chances are you will relax and give yourself longer than 24 hours to adjust.

- Next, remember that the transition process is temporary. There will be a point when you feel comfortable and confident again. For many, being laid off from a job unexpectedly is one of the most devastating situations that occur in their lives. Remember, if it happens to you, it won't last forever. The amount of energy you put into finding your next meaningful work has a direct impact on how you view this situation, how others view you, and how long it will take you to get readjusted. Action breeds progress.

- The third key is to focus on what *is* working in your life. We have a tendency to have a "pity party" when things don't go the way we want them to. By taking inventory of the positives in your life, you will realize that the temporary setback of losing your job is only one facet of your life — it doesn't negate the remaining positives. For example, you are still healthy, have a great family, food, shelter, bowl a perfect 300 game, can cook up a mean pot of chili — you get the picture.

- Lastly, try the "Worst Case Scenario" method of reasoning. Psychologists have proven time and time again that the vast majority of things we worry about *never* happen. If we focus on what actually *does* happen, we find we have the tools we need to handle any situation without draining our energy with needless worry. Actually picture the worst thing that could possibly happen with your current change. If we go back to the example of losing your job, say you never find work again. What would you do? Would you be homeless? What local services and support groups exist? What is the address of the homeless shelter in your city? OK, now that you have "gone there" and solved that problem, resolve to deal with what actually does happen and let go of the needless worry.

Overall, remember that humans are resilient — we are

built to undergo constant change. Think of some of the transitions you have successfully completed — all of the accomplishments you have achieved. The best indicator of how your future will develop is how you have lived your past. Look at your track record and all of the changes you have survived to date. You might even agree that many of these changes have opened the way for improved situations.

Change is challenging, but consider the alternative. Lack of change means lack of growth and lack of, well — life.

# CHAPTER TWO

## *Self-Assessment – Who Are You?*

# Plotting Your Course

---

*"Do what you love and
the money will follow."*

— *Marsha Sinetar*

---

"*A* change will do you good . . ." Maybe so . . . but one of the most difficult transition areas is the work realm. The days of staying comfortable with the same company for 30-40 years have gone the way of polyester bellbottoms and leisure suits. There are still some out there, but do you really want to find them? Like all trends, some of the old rules may return, though they can never be the same. The set of rules that used to apply in the world of work will now include new updates and will have lost some of their original meaning all together. So how do you stay current and get the direction and information you need to succeed?

First, remember that unless you have your own career plan and stay on the path to achieve your goals, you will be a pawn in someone else's plan, helping them to achieve their goals. The step of setting goals is a big one. The percentage of people who achieve their goals is directly proportionate to those who write them and have measurable benchmarks for assessment. And as simple as it may sound, only about 5% of Americans have written life goals.

The key is to get smart about our talents and learn how to thrive within the new system. If you haven't spent some time lately on your career planning goals, now is the best time to start! Grab your pen and spend some time thinking about the keys of career planning.

## Skills

Start by writing all of your jobs, along with the skills you used in each one. A skill is defined as a learned capability such as programming a computer, speaking a foreign language, balancing the books. What patterns do you see? What skills have you outgrown and need to leave behind? Assess areas that you may need to develop. For example, if your technical skills are high, do you need to develop people skills?

Next, create an up-to-date list of the skills and tasks you really enjoy. Consider your current position by taking a look at the tasks that motivate you and make you want to tackle your work each day with enthusiasm. If the job you currently perform doesn't make use of those skills the majority of the time, you may need to look at a change. In the meantime, start looking for opportunities to use those talents in your personal life, on a volunteer basis.

Now it is time to start documenting accomplishments achieved while using your favorite skills. For example, if you listed financial skills, create a list of the budgets you designed, records of how you reduced uncollected debt, reports you developed to track cash flow, etc. Put numbers to the outcomes, so you know the value you bring to your company by increasing profits, saving costs and streamlining processes.

This is one of the most difficult tasks, as we tend to downplay our accomplishments and write them off as "just doing my job". Check out your performance reviews for ideas and look over past projects. In the future, start a file so you can keep track of them on a weekly basis. I recommend a "kudos" file containing all awards, classes attended, notes from clients, samples of your work, etc. Not only will it help you with your accomplishments—you can pull it out on a bad day to cheer you up!

Now it is time to take a look at organizations where you might market your skills. Develop a list of industries that have a need for your skills. Look through the classified ads for ideas. Who is hiring? What companies are moving into town? What types of industry attract you . . . manufacturing, banking, healthcare, fashion, high tech? What are your hobbies? If you love golf, take a look at the golfing industry. Think about the size of the company and their "off the record" reputation on culture and structure.

This area is different for everyone. If money is currently a key motivator in your work, give more weight to this point. If you need to step back briefly in order to move forward quickly, can your finances handle that? Is there long-term growth in this industry? Can you acquire new skills and increase compensation? Many of the people with whom I work are willing to take a cut in pay for the short term in order to reach their long-term goals.

Check out some salary surveys—there are dozens of them on the Web. In addition, if you are considering relocation, cost of living should be a factor in your wages. Base salary is definitely important, but benefits such as stock and bonuses can dramatically increase your overall compensation.

## Marketing Your Skills

Now that you have created an up-to-date profile, evaluate your current work. If you are not using your favorite skills, consider seeking opportunities within your organization where you can, instead of jumping ship. For example, if you work in operations and want to use your skills and knowledge in the marketing arena, volunteer to head up the United Way Campaign; then create a plan that will benefit the company and showcase your skills at the same time.

If you decide to check out external opportunities, set up some informational interviews for learning firsthand about specific companies, trends, compensation, skills and so on. Chat with neighbors, clients, vendors, peers and yes, even your barber — they may know someone in the industry you are researching. This will bring you new contacts and hands-on information.

The final and most important key to career planning is remembering that it is not a task with a beginning and end. Once we get on the wheel of work, it will continue to cycle with or without us. If you do change positions, your first goal will be to update your resume and let your network know your whereabouts. The good news about all of the changes in the working world is that finally, **we** are in charge and have unlimited opportunities to pursue . . . with just a little planning!

# Manifesting Your Destiny

---

*"Destiny is not a matter of chance;*
*It is a matter of choice.*
*It is not a thing to be waited for;*
*it is a thing to be achieved."*

— *William Jennings Bryan*

---

Did you wake up this morning and jump out of bed feeling happy to be alive? Are you excited to see Mondays roll around because your work is part of what makes you thrive? Do you enjoy the city you live in? How about your current relationships — are they working for you?

## Are You Taking the Path of Least Resistance?

Today, we have more tools and technology, freedoms and opportunities than ever before. From my perspective, this means that we have even more incentive to reach our highest goals and create the future we want for ourselves. In reality, I am amazed at the large numbers of people I come into contact with who are just biding their time. People who are simply tired. Choosing to take whatever comes along because it is simply the path of least resistance and can be done effortlessly.

In my work as an executive coach and speaker, I often meet people who say "it's obvious that you love your work—your enthusiasm is boundless!" It is a terrific reality check for me, as I too have worked in the past energetically at jobs I didn't enjoy. I too have experienced failed relationships and have lived in cities that just didn't "feel right". So how do we go from discontent to absolute nirvana? How do we pull out from a slump to get back into the positive zone? Ahh, that is the easy part—if you are willing to get out of the slump, you've done half of the work. All you need to do now is act!

## We Become What We Believe

We create our own reality. I am sure you have heard before that our reality is created by our perceptions. This explains why a comic like Robin Williams, who is considered to be a genius at his craft, has stated that he has a fear that his next joke just won't be funny. That he will use up his talent. Or why extremely thin people sometimes see themselves as obese. What we *believe* is what we see in our minds. And ultimately, that is what we become.

There are endless ways to create your own future. A few strategies that have worked for me may work for you too.

Be willing to do the work required to make change happen. More than one person has looked blankly at me when I've made this statement. We definitely choose the more difficult path when we choose to follow our dreams. It takes sacrifices, introspection, research, and even pain to begin to live your ideal life. There is no jumping ahead just because you want something a lot!

I like the idea of instant gratification, and I admit that more than once I have expected things to just happen. I've learned that unless I take steps to change my behaviors, my results will never change. It's been said that a sign of insanity is continuously doing the same thing over and over and expecting different results. If this sounds like your strategy, it may be time to try a different tactic!

Step into your own power. This statement says it all. The idea of being a victim of circumstances or unable to take steps because of our current situation is guiltily attractive to many of us. It gives us "permission" to take the easy road yet forces us to view ourselves as powerless. Powerless people are slaves to others. Remember, you always have a choice! When we take complete responsibility for our situation and decide what outcome we want, we can begin strategizing.

I have learned that the adage "if it is to be, it is up to me" is absolutely on target. Once you take responsibility for making things happen, the results that you desire will start occurring.

Get over the "Yeahbut" syndrome. The habit of answering every idea with "Yeahbut" is an extremely difficult habit to break, especially for those of us who think we are pretty knowledgeable and experienced. When we find ourselves in a rut, it is often because we are knocking down every idea before it can even be thought through or tried on.

In my career transition work with individuals, it becomes clear to me very quickly whether or not a person is going to default to their old behaviors and continue in a track they do not enjoy or move their wheel to a different groove. There are no mistakes . . . if something doesn't work, you have eliminated that notion and are free to try something else. Listen honestly to yourself — are you shooting down every idea that comes your way? Our knowledge and experience can get in the way of our ability to look at a situation with "new eyes". We are convinced that if it were possible we would have done it already. Try "humoring" a few ideas that you have rejected in the past and see where they lead you now.

Start Now. Nobody said it better than Nike: "Just Do

It!" Thinking you will get around to it when you get your next bonus, the kids are grown, the house is paid off, yadda, yadda, yadda will bring you exactly what you deserve . . . nothing. Stir up the courage to take a step each day and before you know it, you will have created change that adds up to big differences!

# Ten Key Transferable Skills

Technical skills are important and, increasingly, so are the "soft" skills needed to get a job done. For today's workplace, my picks for the most marketable are:

1. **Communications** — the ability to give, receive and share information in all forms to ensure clear understanding.
2. **Customer Focus** — the ability to support the vital link of your customers and ensure that their business is retained while new customers are won.
3. **Problem Solving** — using your talents to bring potential solutions to the table and address all challenges as they occur.
4. **Self-development** — accurately assessing your own strengths and weaknesses, and taking steps in order to improve or compensate.
5. **Initiative** — the ability to take independent action to increase profits, streamline processes and bring in new business.
6. **Comfortableness with Ambiguity** — the ability to learn while doing and change courses rapidly when business dictates.
7. **Embracing Diversity** — the ability to work effectively with people representing all levels of experience, education, power, different cultures, etc.
8. **Teamwork** — the ability to build and maintain positive relationships both inside and outside of your work group.

9. **Technological Savvy** — the ability to confidently navigate the net, create your own presentations and effectively use e-mail.
10. **Organizational Awareness** — the ability to understand how the influence process works, and use it fairly and with integrity.

# CHAPTER THREE

*Growing Yourself and Expanding Your Horizons*

# Recruiting Your Perfect Mentors

---

*You've got to be careful whom you pattern yourself after because you're likely to become just like them."*

— *Rich Mayo*

---

A favorite toy I cherished as a child was called "Mr. Mentor". It was a plastic figure shaped like what seemed to be a real smart guy. I could ask any question, pull his head forward, and the answer popped up on a little viewing screen. Yep, even as a kid, I realized that it never hurt to get some input from another source.

A "Mentor" defined as a tutor, guide or instructor can be anyone you know though your contacts. You probably have contacts both in and outside of your organization that you admire for some reason. They can play a pivotal role in your career development. There will be endless opportunities for your mentors to learn from their association with you as well.

## Mentor vs. Coach

Typically, a coach works with someone for a limited time period on several areas of competency. Mentoring really addresses the big picture and the long term. A mentor may be in your corner for years and through many phases of your career. They may be your role models and give you feedback in broader areas.

A mentor is there to advise and motivate you, but not "do the work" for you. Each and every one of us has to do our own work, look within and make decisions and mistakes to move forward. If your mentor rescues you when you are in the deep water, it may be time to look at that relationship. Advice is great, contacts are helpful, but no one else can learn *your* lessons.

Here are four roles to seek in your own perfect mentors:

**Role Model.** Who do you admire out there? Who has a style of presenting themselves that you find professional, appealing and closely aligned with how you envision yourself? There is a lot to be said for rubbing shoulders with those you most want to be like.

Gender, age, education, role, personal background and experience are a few of the facets impacting the value of a role model to you. Seek role models who embody the traits and values you aspire to live. When we look for opposites in mentors, we end up learning much more than we would in any formal school.

For several years, I mentored a French international business student. She had a terrific academic track record, but no hands on experience. And, while her English was excellent, she did not have the necessary business vocabulary or confidence level. When I hired her as an intern, first we decided what the primary outcomes of the relationship looked like to both of us. We then teamed together to make sure she was connected up to the right people and experiences. By living through my business mistakes and successes, she listened and avoided quite a few potholes in her own career.

**Open — Minded Confidant.** Everyone needs someone to whom they can confidentially vent. And we are not typically looking for someone to solve our problems. Bringing closure or working through a situation is a process. Talking about it out loud to an interested party . . . rather than just in your head . . . is a critical part of the process.

With changes in companies happening at a head-spinning pace, many of us don't feel confident talking openly with coworkers about our problems, vulnerabilities and politics. A mentor will listen without judging you. And if your mentor truly has your best interests in mind, will *not* advise you on actions to take — just offer options.

Confidentiality is one of the reasons most people benefit from building several long-term relationships outside of their own company. Also, not being bogged down within the organization is another benefit to outside mentors.

**Brainstorming Partner.** One of the easiest things to see in others is their unique talents and opportunities for using these talents to their benefit. The theory of GroupThink embraces the proven fact that when a group of people thinks together and brainstorms to a common end, they are collectively smarter than any *one* member of the group.

In my career coaching practice, after meeting a new client for the first time and learning about their situation, I throw out options that have flashed into my mind. I come up with these options based upon what pops up when they talk about skills they love, accomplishments they are proud of and obstacles they face. A third party with no vested interest in the outcome can be far more creative about possibilities. When we put our biases, stereotypes and "yeah buts", on the back burner, the world opens up.

**Honest, Constructive Advisor.** We all know the dreaded feeling of delivering "bad" news to someone. I have coached dozens of top-level managers on how to deliver the message to their employees that they are going to be laid off. While a leader may become more comfortable communicating effectively in these types of situations, they should never become "easy" to deliver.

We are all guilty at one time or another of hedging, or avoiding being totally direct. Maybe a colleague has a distracting habit that they are unaware of. Rather than "embarrass" them, we tend to not mention it . . . except when talking with others about it! Being honest and direct about things that *can be changed* is one of the most useful pieces of feedback we can offer. Someone who takes the time and effort to tactfully deliver information about us and our habits should be respected and the information they provide should provide listened to. Once the information has been heard, we have total choice over whether we make changes or just put the advice in our tool chest for future reference.

Advance your career and your joy level at work by seeking out and asking for support from chosen mentors. Look for advice from numerous sources — it's unrealistic to expect any one person to be able to meet all of your needs. Be curious. Ask. Listen. Learn. And you will Grow!

# Eight Steps to Keeping Your Career Vital

---

*"In the long run you hit only what you aim at, therefore AIM HIGH."*

*— Henry David Thoreau*

---

You are likely spending at least a third of your life working. If we add the commute and time spent thinking about work during your personal time, it is probably closer to two-thirds of your time—right? Since work occupies such a dramatic portion of your time and your life, it should always challenging, stimulating and rewarding. But how can you step back and honestly assess your career? To ensure that you're always in demand and never become extinct, you must change and adapt your skills and work focus to fit the current business environment.

From my perspective, there are eight critical areas in strategizing a vital career. Notice the word "vital"— meaning alive and meaningful—not a career that is just limping along. Let's take a look at some strategies to stretch yourself and enjoy your career in times of perpetual change.

## Research the Marketplace

- If you have been in your current position longer than, say five years, it is time to take a look at the new rules. In today's market, employees are responsible for their own career paths. Ask yourself:
- Are new types of work opening up that will demand my skills?
- Is outsourcing commonplace in my industry?
- What is the turnover rate of workers in my field?
- What companies are setting up shop in my community?
- Are they rolling out new products?
- Are they building a new site?

By looking at approaching trends, you can be on top of the wave when it arrives, instead of having it crash on top of you.

## Know Where You Fit

Where do you fit within the work world? You are more likely to find a great fit where you are most comfortable. Take an inventory and write down what your down the ideal work environment, company size and management style is. Consider:

- Do you work better alone or within a team?
- What are your core values?
- Do you enjoy interfacing directly with customers or like being behind the scenes?
- What size company works best for you?
- What type of management style do you best respond to?
- Is it important that your work make a "difference in the world"?

## Assess Your Portable Skills

Next, make a list of your key skills, ranking them in order of how much you enjoy performing them. (Some people are extremely competent at things they absolutely do not enjoy.) When we change jobs, we take our skills and experience with us. Don't accept a position requiring skills that you can perform in your sleep. New jobs are created every day, so by continually upgrading your skill and experience base, you will be on top of the heap. Now, research the value of the key skills you are selling to ensure fair compensation.

## Track Your Accomplishments

One of the comments I often hear from staffing professionals is that people cannot clearly and concisely state their skills and accomplishments. If we downplay our achievements, we downplay our unique work approach, which is often our most marketable point.

To track your achievements:

- Document when you saved time, money or other resources.
- Determine when you solved a problem or implemented a new idea.
- Be able to talk about your successes in terms of quantifiable results such as by what percent did you reduce operational costs?
- Create an extensive file containing details of all of your projects, courses completed, recognition awards, etc.

## Create a Topnotch Resume

Your resume is your sales brochure, not your life story. You have no doubt seen a variety of opinions on the number of resumes you need and how long they should be. The current trend is for your "marketing piece" to cover the last 10-15 years of your work experience. It should not exceed two pages and most effectively begins with a profile or summary of your skills and experience.

The body of the resume covers your work history, highlighting your accomplishments with bulleted statements. You need to back up your summary statement throughout your resume with concise fact statements highlighting examples of your successes. Remember to emphasize the skills you are selling—the ones you enjoy the most and want to develop even more. If your resume contains examples of projects you have done well in the past but no longer want to do, you are sending a mixed message to the hiring company.

## Script Your 30-Second Commercial

Networking—exchanging information with others—is the name of the game, so prepare an interesting overview of who you are and what you do best. Use this professional introduction for times by chance or design, that you are speaking with others about your work. Your commercial should include types of work you do, industries in which you have experience and your key skills. Add several personality traits, as well as some of your motivators and accomplishments. Whenever you are asked, "Tell me a little bit about yourself", you will have done your advance preparation, clearly stating what makes you unique. When you exploit your skills to the benefit of other people, you can't help but succeed, so don't keep your talents to yourself!

## Evaluate Your Attitude

Most of us tend to take life too seriously. You are the Mistress, the Master, the King, the Queen of your mind. No one can get inside your head if you do not allow it. When we look at each day as a new beginning, we are open to opportunities that come our way. Things could always be worse. Remember to smile when you come into contact with others and use humor to help ease the stress we all feel. Encourage those around you and support them in meeting their goals. If you ask for what you need, you will have a dramatically increased probability of getting it!

## Set Your Goals

This is probably the easiest but most neglected point. If you are on a road with no goals, you are on somebody else's map. The more ambiguous the times, the more crystal clear you need to be about what *you* want. Write down your goals; then write the steps you are willing to take to make them happen. If you hesitate to write them down because goals change, make it a practice to adjust them as you go. Without goals, we are just on one long road trip with no destination. Write your tangible, measurable, realistic goals, and your success ratio will skyrocket!

I challenge you to view these points as a reality check. How can you ensure your career success in the next decade? *You* are in charge! Know your goals and have fun reaching them. It is your decision whether your road will be smooth or full of potholes!

# Building Your Professional Network

---

*"Help your brother to climb the hill and you will find yourself nearer the top."*

*— Unknown*

---

It's finally your time to wow the world! You've got dozens of copies of your killer resume and have even invested in an "interview suit". You answer ads, but nothing is happening. You are not even getting the obligatory rejection letters. Doubt sets in, and you just *know* it is because you lack experience.

The problem may be that you are spending too much time sending out resumes and not enough time *talking* to people. Statistics show that more than 75% of jobs are landed through networking, but YOU just don't know anybody. Building a network takes years, right?

## Why Network?

Your professional network is one of your most powerful assets and building it should continue throughout your entire career. To define the word, look at it as "information exchange", with people exchanging ideas, resources and contacts to support one another in reaching goals. Let's take a look at *why* you need to network:

- You need to get the word out about your availability, qualifications and objectives
- You're seeking information about your target market
- You want details about specific companies
- You're in need of general career advice
- You're in the market for "sponsors" — people who can talk to others about how great you are
- You're looking for referrals and introductions to hiring managers in other organizations

## What Networking Will Bring You

Think of networking as talking with people to get *advice and information and referrals* — not to *ask them for a job.* Looking at things from that perspective will take some of the pressure off right away. You will be exchanging information. Remember — you are now in the market and will have lots of information to offer in return. If you really don't have any information to offer in return, be a great listener and offer your ear to people who like to talk about heir own accomplishments.

Networking will be your version of baiting traps. With some contacts, you may "catch" information of no use to you or you may come up empty. With others, you may just lose your bait. But an important percentage of them will come up with information, interviews and valuable contacts.

## You're Already Doing It

To make the idea of networking a little easier to digest, consider how much you have been networking over the past four years. You have probably asked others for information such as:

- Which classes are the best to sign up for?
- Which professors are best?
- Which clubs have the best bands?
- Who has a used car for sale?
- Who knows somebody driving to LA when you need a ride?
- You need two more tickets for the game—whom do you call?

Networking is simply a way of sharing information about common goals.

## Getting Your Act Together

A common networking mistake is being unsure of what you want—which means others really can't help you. Before you begin networking, take time to outline your objective, qualifications and goals, as well as the companies you want to target for employment. Perfect your resume and be ready to participate in any opportunity that comes your way. Forget the idea of finding a position because you are "lucky." Good luck has a tendency to show up when you are prepared for any situation!

## Tap In to Your Friends and Family

To start networking, make a list of everyone you can possibly think of, such as: friends, family members, neighbors, professors, hair stylist, dentist and mechanic. Include contacts from your part-time jobs over the years, religious organizations and your gym. No contact is off-limits. After all, networking is a two-way street and you will be looking for information that could benefit them as well!

Give the people on your list a call or send them a short e-mail letting them know your goals, key skills and target companies. Invite them to give you advice. If they offer, send them a copy of your resume.

## Business Cards

Regardless of where you get them — the Internet, your local copy center or printing establishment — you need to invest in business cards. The $20 expenditure will put you on a level playing field with professionals who give their cards out as a part of their professional identity. Your card should include your full name, phone number and e-mail address. If you want, list your area of specialty, such as Information Technology or Organizational Development. The next time someone gives you a business card, instead of looking for something to write your number on, you can just pull out one of your business cards.

## Professional Associations

To learn the ways of the business world, start attending as many professional meetings as you possibly can. Check the library, the Internet or local publications for a listing of associations. *The Business Journal*, a weekly publication specific to your neighborhood, always includes a listing of meetings.

You need not be a member to attend, nor do you need an invitation. Just call for a reservation and make sure you get there early. A networking portion typically precedes the formal meeting. This is where you circulate and ask questions. What skills are needed in their industry? How do they go about recruiting talent? What trends are impacting their business?

Hand out your business cards to each person you speak with and thank them for their information. If they give you one of their cards, make notes on the back of it later to remember exactly who they are. Consider how you might connect with them at a later time.

When you find an organization that you enjoy, make it a point to join. Then begin showing your stuff by volunteering. Arrive ahead of schedule to help with setting up, making nametags or distributing handouts. Your personal traits will shine through, and you will begin to build trust and a reputation of following through.

Remember, networking does not mean begging, asking for something or owing people. It does mean establishing relationships while participating in activities you love. Offer to help others in meeting their goals as you pave the way to realizing your own dreams. When you spend time networking without a sense of being owed something, your confidence will increase and your competition for positions will rise.

The movie "Six Degrees of Separation" immortalized the theory that we are all separated by only six contacts. Based upon this, you will be amazed at how many quick phone calls result in terrific connections. So get on the network bandwagon and start helping others to meet their goals — the benefits will come back to you tenfold!

# Make Money, Make Friends, Be A Success

---

*"In order to get what you've never had, do what you've never done."*

*— Unknown*

---

One of the most wonderful things about being part of this big learning realm we call "work" is that we have unlimited choices. We can never really make a "wrong choice" because every path leads us to new opportunities and valuable experiences.

While we all need to make our own mistakes, here are a few things I wish I had known at the *start* of my career:

## Lessons Learned

- **Have a positive attitude.** This is an absolute make-or-break trait. The good and bad news is that only *you* are the boss of your mind. There is absolutely no way to be influenced by others *unless you allow it*. It is so easy to be pessimistic, taking the stance that you are the victim of one negative circumstance after another. If you view each situation as an opportunity to learn, it is much easier to realize why you are experiencing it. Choose to be positive.

- **Be an encourager.** From a very early age, we are programmed to accept others' standards as our own. And we often feel that we don't measure up. In fact, psychologists state that by the time we start school, over 90% of us have been made to feel inadequate. Look for ways to help others feel appreciated, recognized and encouraged. Seek out their uniqueness and help them develop these gifts.
- **Exploit your strengths** to the benefit of others and you will be wildly successful. Find out what really motivates you. Appraise your most valued skills and determine how they can be used to help others succeed. When you are part of others' success, your own returns are phenomenal. Leave a legacy of making a positive impact on the lives of others.
- **Listen to your internal voice.** More importantly, heed what you hear. If you feel stagnant in a job and know it is time to move on . . . *do it*. Don't keep thinking about what might happen. We usually know what's best for us. If we would just tune in and act on what we innately know, we could skip many steps in the progress ladder. Too often, we rely on advice from others and overlook the voice that knows us best — our own.
- **Put things into perspective.** Nothing can be considered permanent. When we realize that most of our experiences have pros and cons, we can be a little less attached to outcomes. Things could be worse, or they could be better.

Learn how to put a positive spin on a negative situation. It makes news easier to digest, gives you a quicker readjustment focus and sure beats the alternative.

- **Volunteer your talents.** Regardless of age, education, importance or experience level, everyone has talents. Share them generously with people, organizations, missions and causes in which you believe. And don't keep track as you go along. You might give and give for decades, never getting anything back. Then again, you may find that you have built your own network of valuable supporters.

- **Delight in differences.** Human nature dictates that we naturally gravitate toward others like ourselves. Managers hire people with whom they feel comfortable and share something in common. Instead, try seeking out and delighting in differences. You can multiply your learning when you tune in to what others have to say.

- **Ask for feedback.** If you ever get to the point that you think you have everything figured out and are confident with the answers — run, don't walk, for feedback from trusted advisors. It can be dangerous allowing yourself to become insulated against input from those who know your overall game plan. You may be living in a bubble!

- **Take calculated risks.** Look for opportunities to stretch your skills and responsibilities. We generally don't want to make changes unless we absolutely have to. In other words, when we are more uncomfortable with accepting things the way they are than entering unknown territory, we make changes. And when we discover we have waited too long, changes sometimes "happen" without our buying in to them. Taking a calculated risk means weighing pros and cons and potential losses or wins *before* making big changes.

- **Take care of *you* first.** The idea of always putting your own needs last is wonderfully noble . . . it is also a dead-end street. When your own needs are met, you are far more valuable to others. "Put your own oxygen mask on first" before attempting to help anyone else. When you are drained, you can't contribute in any way. Invest in yourself and you will see your personal "stock" go way up in everyone's eyes — most importantly, your own.

- **Never stop learning.** We have all felt the exhilaration of graduating from *something*. Ah, you've learned it all. Resting awhile is a terrific feeling. But the next time a new book is written or a new study published, we are out of date again. So don't ever stop learning or you will become extinct.

- **Capitalize on trends.** Going back to the idea of change, keep a diligent eye on the trends driving the globe, your chosen industry and the competition. Avoid getting bogged down resisting; figure out how you can use the trend to get closer to your goals. It worked for those making whiskey during prohibition and will continue to work until the end of time — the theory of supply and demand!

Everyone makes his or her own journey. Again, there are no wrong decisions — just different paths and lessons. We can choose to have fun in the process or not. Take a risk . . . have fun with it!

# Emotional Intelligence—
# Your Key To Success

---

*"He who knows others is learned;*
*he who knows himself is wise."*

— *LAOTSE, The Character of Tao*

---

Intelligence. IQ Scores. National Norms. From an early age, we learn that we are judged in comparison to others to determine how "smart" we are. Think back to the first time that you learned the results of some sort of test you had taken. How did it feel? Like you were brilliant? A loser? Average? Were you competitive?

I can recall always feeling as if I was bright enough, but not *gifted*. As I got older, I started to feel less "smart" in some circumstances. For instance, others could play a game like Trivial Pursuit® and spiel off dates, names, rivers . . . whatever . . . much more accurately than I. Then, one day I heard about Daniel Goleman's book *"Emotional Intelligence"*.

## Daniel Goleman's Theory

Goleman's writings describe "emotional intelligence" as "the capacity for recognizing our own feelings and those of others, for motivating ourselves, and for managing emotions well in ourselves and in our relationships".

HOO-ah! All of the sudden, I felt SMART! I readily embraced his philosophy and still emphasize its importance in my work with clients in transition. Basically, it says that true intelligence is a *combination* of the head (mental quality) and the heart (emotional quality). Hence, the name "Emotional Intelligence (EQ)".

## "Street Smarts"

You see, my own life experience included living abroad, frequently transferring schools and having to assimilate to a new pace— moving over 20 times by college graduation. I had attended high school in three countries and was confident in my social skills. I realized that I was much more tolerant of differences than many of my newfound friends who had lived in the same town their entire lives. As it has turned out, what I knew as my "street smarts"—having common sense and the ability to figure things out by doing—were actually some of my most valuable skills in both my business and personal relationships.

## EQ as a Competitive Edge

I have often observed that the difference between employees that were labeled "average" and those that were labeled "stars" had a lot to do with EQ. The ability to depersonalize— or take the pride out of—situations and do what is best for the team was a factor. The attitude of looking over, under or around obstacles and remaining positive and motivated after failures was a huge indicator of an employee's overall success with an organization.

## EQ is Important

If this is starting to sound like you . . . great! Remind yourself of the importance of these skills and continue to develop them. If you are realizing that this is an area you may want to develop, then read on!

Walter Mischel a researcher at Columbia University tested a group of four-year olds for their ability to resist temptation and hold out for rewards. He found that those most successful in the experiment were much more successful in their lives and careers. Goleman's work supports that people of average intelligence and high emotional intelligence do surprisingly well in comparison to those who have *only* a high IQ. One's ability to recognize advantage through resisting short-term gain for long-term payoff is an indicator of high EQ.

Think about it . . . did you ever have a teacher who was absolutely brilliant . . . but always forgot their keys? Or what time class was scheduled to begin? This is why there is absolutely no correlation between formal education and success on the job . . . or in life. It's all in the *application* of what we learn.

## What's YOUR EQ?

If you are curious and would like to take a quick Emotional Quotient (EQ) test, there are dozens available on the web. I tried the one at: http://www.queendom.com/tests/emotionaliq.html

I found that the results summary was remarkably insightful and reminded me of several areas that I tend to neglect.

## "Soft Skills" Sell!

It is no secret that the best projects, promotions and recognition go to those who step up to the plate. Our current work environment demands that we are competent in the area of "soft skills" — that we don't take constructive feedback as personal criticism. We need to tune into the big picture and larger goals . . . not only our own personal goals and responsibilities.

## Know What Makes YOU Tick

Take time to accurately assess your strengths and weaknesses. Be aware of your limits and take time to celebrate and assess your accomplishments as well! Reflect on where you might want to put some energy to develop additional skills. If you are serious about increasing your EQ, put yourself in stretch situations.

I spent over five years on the road on work related assignments. I never felt comfortable dining alone in a restaurant. When I thought about *why*, I realized that the feeling was 90% my own reaction to the situation . . . not the situation itself. Most . . . OK, none . . . of the things that I was uncomfortable with happened anyway. These days, I never hesitate to ask for a specific table, I bring along a small notebook in case I have any thoughts I want to record and have a ball looking at everyone else. I actually enjoy being served and definitely deserve it after a long day in a strange city.

A high score on your Emotional Intelligence Quotient won't necessarily make you one of Regis' Millionaires, but your life, relationships and career will be much more fun and fulfilling! listen, learn. And you will grow!

# Time: Make The Most Of It

---

*"Spend everyday casual, but industrious;*
*Every moment alert, but relaxed."*

— *Guy Finley*

---

Yesterday is a canceled check — we can never get that time back. And tomorrow? A promissory note — it may never come. Today, yes *today*, is cash — and we have to spend it wisely by the end of the day, or it will be gone forever. Time is one thing we all seem to spend a lot of our lives thinking and talking about — mostly how we have "too little of it". Since we have a limited supply of time, the obvious answer is to rethink the idea that we need more of it and concentrate on "making more" out of it.

## Using a Reminder System

The most important foundation for effective time management is a reminder system. With dozens of things to remember each week, we quickly become overwhelmed with an entire year of events. Check out some of the new organization systems available. These will do the remembering and sometimes the reminding for you. Is it time for you to invest in a hand-held computer? Is it a hassle to have a separate calendar for work and for personal activities? Are you still doing just fine with 3 x 5 cards in your pocket? Develop your own reminder system—when you become more organized, your track record of getting things done on time will soar ... and it will seem that you are "creating" more time overall.

## Daily Plan

Write out your plan each day. List the top ten tasks you commit to accomplish. The more *flexible* you make your schedule, the more time you will *waste*. Schedule in time for unexpected events, your personal exercise time, and even time to communicate with friends and family. Our personal time is what we usually lose when we run short, so don't forget to include it on *every* day's schedule. The balance created between work and play will give you extra stamina and make you a more pleasant person to be around.

If you are a more unstructured type, try breaking your day into three segments and writing down what you need to accomplish in each part without pinning down an exact time.

## Creative Thinking

Everyone needs an hour early in the day without interruptions. This is when you will review recent activity, develop long-term goals and list the steps you need to take to reach them. If you do your thinking when you are at your best, you can jot short notes to yourself during the rest of the day and refer back to them later. The strategy that works best for me is to get up an hour earlier than I need to accomplish my regular morning tasks. It gives me the opportunity to ease into the day, journal, answer correspondence and start the day fresh.

# Multi-task

Multi-task! When you are doing routine things, add in an extra step. For example, read the newspaper or business periodicals when you are on the treadmill, return phone calls on your "hands-free" phone while driving, or listen to motivational tapes while you cook dinner. We are wired to handle many tasks simultaneously — so keep developing this skill. Draw the line when you are meeting with other people and give them your full attention. For example, don't work on the computer while you are talking to someone on the phone. Time gained doesn't make up for rudeness!

When faced with a group of tasks, do the most dreaded first. Your enthusiasm level will be higher, and it will all be downhill from there. Nothing is worse than having to muster up the gusto to do the thing you dread most at the end of a long day.

# Paperwork

You have probably heard this one before — "Handle each piece of paper only once". This is a simple, but difficult thing to do. I suggest this method combined with a *few, thick* files — one for bills to be paid at a later time, one for letters to be written, and so on. Paper needs to do either be handled immediately or stored for future reference. There are certainly a lot of things that you can take care of in "real time," such as scanning newsletters and either filing or tossing, responding to e-mails, etc.

# Avoid Interruptions

When expecting visitors, set a definite time — both at work and at home. At work, beware of drop-ins. Watch out for the lack of planning on someone else's part creating a time crisis for you! Communicate, and gently let others who are running behind schedule know if this impacts your schedule, too. If you are in the middle of an important project, let the phone ring and check voice mail at your earliest convenience. How many times were those voice mails actually emergencies, anyway? This will not only help you focus, but you'll also make fewer errors.

## Meetings

A meeting can be a terrific tool for communication and training. The trick is to have it organized in advance. Create an agenda and distribute it to all attendees before the meeting time, when possible. Build in some discretionary time for green-light thinking and some structured time. Start at the designated time. Try recruiting a volunteer at each meeting to take brief notes and distribute to attendees within 24 hours with follow-up items. The note-taking role at my meetings is delegated to the last person who enters the room, so it is sometimes passed to several people, but does encourage getting there on time!

For successful time management, the little things are what you need to manage most closely. By keeping a close eye on your schedule every day, you will find that it is a breeze to get things done. Take control of your time . . . before *it* controls *you*!

# Top Ten Time-Wasters

1.  **Handling a piece of paper multiple times** — Take care of it the *first* time around, or put it in a specific file for follow-up.
2.  **Forgetting to re-prioritize** — With many interruptions during the day, we need to step back and evaluate when it is time to change priorities.
3.  **Procrastinating** — Postponing the inevitable is a terrible burden to carry around — do it *now*!
4.  **Working from memory** — Select a reminder system that works for your own pace and lifestyle — then use it!
5.  **Telephone Interruptions** — The phone is a tool — control when you answer it and how long you stay on it.
6   **Overbooking** — Failure is in the making when we attempt too much at once and underestimate the time needed to do things.
7.  **Lack of clear goals** — With a great plan and steps to get there, you will streamline time and avoid having to start over.
8.  **Visitors** — Prepare for people who drop in unexpectedly and linger way too long.
9.  **Clutter** — A messy work and home area means lost items and lost time to locate them when needed.
10. **Fear of saying "No"** — Be selective with how you spend your time, as well as the people you allow to take time away from your schedule. It's OK to decline sometimes!

# Simplify Your Life!

*"The trouble with the rat race is that even if you win you're still a rat."*

— Lily Tomlin

It seems like almost every periodical I pick up these days is full of advice and information on how to do things quicker, better, faster. I've been compliant . . . and found that I had fallen into the trap of carrying a cell phone, pager, laptop . . . whatever. After all, we've gotta stay available and plugged in to be competitive!

When I brought in the last New Year, I officially made a conscious decision to simplify my life. That has meant making some tough choices regarding my time, interaction with others, buying habits and well, virtually every facet of my life. In short, I am building my own new set of principles. Here are a few of my favorite strategies for simplifying your life.

## Schedule Less—Not More

List Making has long been a pastime—and at this stage, I rely on my daytimer and task lists to keep my life up to date. Trouble was, I had a longtime habit of scheduling way more than even Wonder Woman could have accomplished. At the end of each day, I wasn't exactly feeling successful as I viewed my list with half of the items left undone.

Now, I create a rolling list that changes daily. It begins with a list of tasks with time sensitive deadlines. It may be getting my car inspected, meeting a colleague for lunch or completing a project proposal. My second list contains all of the other items to be completed as time allows. A sort of cafeteria plan—I just select items that I am in the mood to complete within my available time frame. This way, at the end of the day, my list of priority tasks has been completed and I start fresh each day.

## View the Phone as a Tool

At one time, the phone was primarily used to relay important information or handle emergencies. Ignoring a ringing phone was definitely not in my programming. Fact is, the phone has become not a tool, but a means of telemarketing, idle communication and often, a tremendous time waster.

My newly adopted strategy is to simply rely on voice mail and view the phone as a valuable tool. I soon learned that the world didn't come to an end when I left the cell phone at home. Now I return calls and respond to messages during a block of time instead of stopping every five minutes for an interruption and losing my focus. People are getting better about leaving concise messages, that allow for a voice or email return answer. The result has been that I get far more done, avoid long useless conversations and almost always miss the telemarketers! I don't go so far as caller ID or screening calls—it's all about the luck of the draw. My concentration and output has risen dramatically.

## Learn to Love Saying "NO"

Being able to say "no" without feeling guilty is another biggie. You probably know exactly what it feels like to be in demand. To have a reputation of being reliable and dependable and the person to get the job done. This reaction to everyone else's needs builds a never-ending road to an overloaded schedule.

It's not easy to change this behavior, because when others need you to help them take care of THEIR obligations, they can be quite convincing. If you're at all wishy-washy, you'll be sucked in before you know it. Remember, if something isn't on YOUR agenda—an agenda that can reasonably include assisting others on projects pertinent to a team effort—it is leading you down a path to help someone else reach their goals, while yours are left in the dust.

While this adjustment is challenging, it is completely doable—IF you stick to your guns. The more you learn to say "no", the easier it gets and the results will be amazing. You'll soon have plenty of time and will enjoy choosing exactly when and how you want to use it. Now, all those people who used to depend on you to help them get their projects done will either find other people to replace you or learn to do it themselves!

## Beat the Clutter Trap

The strategy of taking care of things as they came and getting the job done "no matter what it takes" worked for me for many years. My strategy was simple—when a task presented itself, I completed it. I soon realized this was not enough and that I needed to schedule time to perform "maintenance".

I now begin each day with 20-30 minutes of filing, putting books and supplies back where they belong, deleting emails and organizing the day. The results include significantly less stress and more room to bring in new resources. Take one day a month to just do maintenance or work on it daily—either way, you'll end up having far more time to get the job done.

The smallest steps add up to big differences. While it may seem that changing the way your organize your work and life is a hassle, you will soon learn that it really pays off. Schedule Less, Love Saying "NO", view the Phone as a Tool and Beat the Clutter Trap. These four strategies will add up to more time and less stress as you Simplify Your Life!

# Opportunity Knocks—
# Are You Home?

---

*"There is no future in any job. The future lies
in the man who holds the job."*

— *George Crane*

---

You are a star performer and your company is offering you career options for the future. They have two positions in mind, and they are pushing you toward one of them. You are really not interested in either. Hmmm. Do you take door number One and stay where you are, or Door Number Two and go where *they* want you to go?

Stretch assignments are what we need to "have a successful career". It is clear that we are responsible for creating our own career path. It is imperative to know where *you* want to end up. As long as you are on *your* path, headed toward *your* goals, you will be successful. If you take an assignment off that path, you become a part of someone else's agenda and goals.

## A Position Created for You

When you are doing a great job, you get noticed. And that means opportunities come your way. When you are prepared and headed toward your own career goals, you will need to evaluate every offer.

Sometimes, management makes a position available to you where they know you will succeed. When that happens, take time to evaluate the situation. If you take it, will you be closer toward your own goals after completing the project? Or, will you be off the path but possibly gain skills that would serve you well in the future? If you want to turn down the project, stick to your decision. Don't be swayed just to please someone else or to be politically correct. In the long run, you will come to resent your employer and lose your sense of loyalty.

## Look at All Your Options

The best way to evaluate options is to make a list of the pros and cons — both long — and short-term. Putting it down on paper will help you sort out your thoughts.

Remember, it's fine to change goals or to make a short-term decision that will help meet a long-term goal. For example, if you can build key relationships or work with a coveted client, which skills you use are not as important. Key players come and go and your professional rapport with them will transfer if either of you leave your current organization.

## Communicate with Your Employer

By passing up opportunities, you can quickly become labeled as someone who does not want additional responsibility or is afraid of change. The best way to handle that issue is to be clear up-front about your goals, as well as the skills you want to use to help the organization reach its goals. If you turn down a position, let management know why — then pay attention to their reaction. Do they try to convince you to take the position because it is best for them? If so, it may be time to consider moving on.

## The Best Ways to Communicate

- Clearly state your intended career goals to management.
- Ask for assignments that will give you the experience you want.
- Elicit their advice.
- Keep them posted of your accomplishments.

## Real-world Examples

At one time, I coached two technical professionals from the same organization. Both were bright, talented and had in-demand skills. The first one complained about being overlooked for the best projects. He whined about lack of opportunity and repeatedly said he was going to leave. But he didn't. Nor did he work at finding a better opportunity. Complaining and taking the assignment anyway won't help you move forward. Don't help the organization meet its goals at your expense.

The other technical professional I coached turned down projects on several occasions, as they did not present the growth opportunities she was seeking. When she turned down an assignment, she reinforced to her manager the skills and technical areas on which she was currently concentrating.

Learn to make your skills known to your employer, especially when it's time for you to take on something new. Communication will help you to enjoy your job and meet your goals.

# CHAPTER FOUR

*Attitude —*
*It's Your Choice*

# The Choice For Optimism

---

*"An optimist sees an opportunity in every calamity; a pessimist sees a calamity in every opportunity."*

*— Winston Churchill*

---

One thing that you and *only* you have 100% control over in this learning exercise called "life" is your mind. That's right, folks. You are the King, the Queen, the Top Dog, the Potentate, the Big Cheese, the Grand Poobah of your mind. Absolutely no one can take away your ability to control your thoughts unless you *let* them! By choosing the path of optimism, you will not only be more successful, but will definitely have more fun "getting there".

In my work, I have often partnered with professionals undergoing career transitions due to someone else's decision. They were generally offshoots of the decade of layoffs and de-installings. The determining factor regarding length of their job search was the attitude that these folks chose to embrace during this chapter of their lives.

## Victim or Opportunist?

At the core of the attitude is the decision to be an optimist or a pessimist. When we see ourselves as victims, our attitudes and energies pull us away from what we need to accomplish, keeping us focused on *who* is at fault. By taking responsibility for our situations, we adopt the attitude of the opportunist—one who can make fine wine from sour grapes.

The English word "crisis" is translated by the Chinese with two characters: one meaning "danger" and the other, "opportunity". This clearly illustrates the point that our actions are absolutely critical in living out situations as either a pessimist or an optimist. The former will not take action— the latter does!

In 1948, Harvard University began a 200-man study measuring optimism vs. pessimism. The results over a 35-year period showed that those who viewed life in an optimistic manner enjoyed better health, more emotional stability, earned more money, had fewer divorces, experienced less drug and alcohol abuse, had fewer symptoms of old age, and even lived longer. Why would you choose pessimism in the face of evidence that it's dangerous to your health?

## The Deciding Factors on Attitude

So, if our attitude is our choice, why do so many people choose the worst? If pessimism is learned, why can't optimism be learned? According to Dr. Martin Seligman, senior researcher and professor of psychology at the University of Pennsylvania, "Optimists and pessimists are made, not born." According to our life experiences, we have observed and then learned to be either an optimist or a pessimist. Seligman, author of "Learned Optimism", states we can unlearn pessimism and train ourselves to be more optimistic.

To accomplish this, you need to consider several areas, known as the Three P's. Is the situation:

- **Permanent?** Do you look at this as a permanent situation, or will it change at some point? At some time, will you recover?

- **Pervasive?** Does it seep over to other parts of your life? That is, does it impact your relationship with your friends, family or your self-esteem?
- **Personal?** Was the event an action against you personally or could it have happened just as easily to someone else?

An example would be experiencing a criminal attack. Consider the scenario of two people being mugged in a city park. While neither was seriously hurt, they reacted very differently.

The first victim viewed it as a random experience, not allowing it to affect other parts of her life. She did not think of it as a personal attack, but a wake-up call to remember to use safety precautions.

The second victim became withdrawn, afraid to leave her apartment alone. She allowed it to affect her mental attitude and productivity at work. In addition, she felt that the robber had been watching her, selected her from a crowd, and would be back to do something even worse the next time.

Needless to say, the chosen reaction of the first victim is far more beneficial.

## Awareness . . . Acceptance . . . Action

The next time you experience an uncomfortable situation, try stepping back to examine your reaction. By controlling your response, you will be able to control the overall outcome. When you become aware of an attitude that will not bring you to your overall goals, you have reached the first step toward changing. Next is the acceptance that you and you *alone* are responsible for the outcome. And thirdly, put together a plan of action with several back-up plans. Enlist the help of others you trust if you are not able to come up with enough options.

*Camille M. Primm*

## Optimistic and Realistic

Being optimistic is *not* about wearing blinders or being unrealistic. It *is* about choices based upon reality and common sense. If a skydiver thinks "Oh well, I think I will jump just this one time without my reserve parachute", that choice is not optimistic. It is just plain stupid.

Life is an adventure. It is definitely much more fun if you believe that you deserve the best and that good things will continue to come your way, even if you have had a string of negative experiences. Choose optimism! I am confident you will enjoy the ride!

# Put Humor In Your Life

---

*"Laughing stirs up the blood, expands the chest, electrifies the nerves, clears away the cobwebs from the brain, and gives the whole system a cleansing rehabilitation."*

— *Unknown*

---

We all know people who have a great time . . . no matter WHAT they are doing. And often, we don't like them for exactly that reason! Humor is a commodity that is absolutely, positively 100% free, and yet few of us take advantage of it. When is the last time YOU laughed at work? Or perhaps more importantly, when is the last time you made others laugh?

Taking life lightly is great advice especially when you consider the tangible benefits. First of all, it takes fewer muscles to smile than to frown . . . and burns more calories. If that doesn't get you thinking, laughter also lowers blood pressure and stimulates the release of endorphins into our bodies. Endorphins are the same stress-relieving agents that are triggered by exercise. Overall, laughter stimulates the immune system and offsets the effects of stress.

## So Why Aren't We Laughing More?

Sometimes we just become too focused to really enjoy the situation we are in at the moment. How many times have you heard the mantra "live in the moment"? It *is* possible to see humor in almost any situation and yet we are often a million miles away from the situation we are actually experiencing. Like the person who goes on vacation only to see it through a camcorder viewfinder. When he gets home, he plays the tape of his vacation and realizes he's watching other people have fun, never having had any of his own.

Somewhere along the line, the message has drifted down that life is serious. We may be concerned that if we make jokes, others will doubt our intelligence write us off as not being serious minded. In reality, most of us admire people who can laugh at themselves or help us to see the humor in a situation.

A university tracked second graders as laughing an average of 247 times a day in contrast to adults laughing only seven times! What is wrong with this picture? Make the choice to look at the light side of life!

## Why Should We Laugh?

So why should we laugh? Apart from the health benefits we already discussed, it's fun to laugh. And, we all know that time flies when we are having fun. It creates a synergy and a sense of excitement in any situation. If you were in a crowded restaurant, which party would you rather join— the one laughing and having fun or the one chatting somberly? Using humor makes people feel relaxed, part of the group and open. It is obvious that it supports building relationships and business partnerships as well!

Robert Half International, a leading staffing company recently conducted a survey of 100 vice presidents of major corporations. Their study revealed that 84% thought employees with a sense of humor performed better than people with little or no sense of humor. Go figure! And you thought work was supposed to be serious!

And you know what else? Another study conducted by interviewing over 700 CEOs, showed 98% as stating they would hire a person with a good sense of humor over someone who lacks a sense of humor. Who would have thought that lack of humor would be a career-limiting trait?

## A Study of Humor

In the late 70's, an individual by the name of Norman Cousins brought attention to the subjects of humor and laughter to the medical community. He had been diagnosed with a serious medical condition and believed that laughter held therapeutic benefits. He believed that negative emotions had a negative effect on health, so therefore the opposite held true as well. Cousins theorized that feelings of hope, joy, confidence and love were byproducts of laughter. His work was significant enough to earn him a position for the last 12 years of his life as a researcher at the UCLA Medical School.

## What Is It OK to Laugh At?

This is an important note, as inappropriate humor can be destructive. The simple guideline is that laughing at anything that CAN be changed is OK. For example, if there is a temporary situation, it is within bounds. Making fun of a person's physical appearance . . . such as their height . . . or lack thereof, *isn't* okay. Creating plays on words or revisiting personal experiences is a great source for humorous stories. A note here about inappropriate jokes about sex, race, etc. Though funny to you, they may not be funny to others. Keep these out of the workplace!

## How Can We Start Laughing More?

If you are having trouble seeing humor in your work situation, picture one of your favorite comedians in the same situation and imagine how *they* would handle it. For example, what do you think Lucille Ball would do if she had two meetings scheduled at the same time and the phone was ringing off the hook? If Jim Carey were trying to meet that deadline while shorthanded and dealing with an incompetent co-worker, what strategy would he use?

Actress Ethel Barrymore once said: "You grow up the day you have your first real laugh, at yourself." The ability to see humor in real life is priceless . . . and there is a never-ending supply of material. Start looking around . . . and live life in the laugh lane!

# A Positive Attitude—
# Your Most Important Asset

---

*"There is very little difference in people.
But that 'little' difference makes
a 'big' difference.
The little difference is attitude.
The big difference is whether it is
positive or negative."*

— *W. Clement Stone*

---

How can we be expected to live positively in a negative world? When we turn on the TV news channel, we see violence all over the world. We read the newspapers and see more crime and tragedy. We go to work and see constant change, mergers, and layoffs.

## Perspective is King!

How can we be positive? The answer is *perspective*. Perspective is the biggest differentiator between those who are seemingly always in a good mood while others are grumpy.

Putting things into perspective starts when you wake up in the morning. Here we go, another day commuting, facing traffic, and meeting deadlines. Consider the alternative . . . some people *didn't* wake up today! And in some parts of the world people woke up in *true* chaos — war, famine or widespread disease. *It could always be worse!*

# You're In Control

If we start with the basics, opting for a positive attitude is actually the easiest choice. YOU are the king, the queen, the Big Cheese of your mind. No one can get inside your head and force you to change your attitude. We all know negative people and they have convinced themselves and try to convince you of the reasons why something *won't* work. Apply the effort spent finding problems to finding solutions and you will come up with at least one good reason why something *will* work . . . so do it! If you can think of a problem, you can think of a solution, simple as that.

Take control and change things within your power. Let the rest of it go. You can listen to negative people, but don't invite their ideas to come in and be a part of your thoughts. Believe me, those negative folks would much rather be in *your* shoes. Rather than try to convince them to be positive, just listen, and move on.

# Choose to Feel Worthy

You are important — regardless of your "role" in life. We all came in equal and are going out equal too. We are all just as important as the next guy is. It is how we perceive our value and the value and quality of our work that determines our ability to feel successful. When you take pride in what you do — no matter how small the task, the benefits will start to pile up.

You may know people who think they are worthier or

deserve more. Fact is, a university study showed that 96% of us feel unworthy in some area before we ever even start school! If we feed these feelings with more evidence, it will be impossible to overcome them. If however, we focus on what we can do well, the scene reverses.

## Know Where You're Headed

Lack of focus and goals is a huge handicap to a positive attitude. When you just go through the motions and don't even know what you are working toward, you never feel a sense of accomplishment. Take time to get clear on what you really want to achieve. Now, decide what you are willing to give up to get it. That's right—you may have to trade off somewhere.

Let's say you are not happy with your work and really want to change careers. You can probably come up with dozens of obstacles including: lack of training in the new area, having to step back financially, or you have no tangible experience in your true area of interest. The longer you wait to make the change, the more uncomfortable you will be. And thinking about it will just take up energy that could be used elsewhere.

Even if you do have to step back temporarily, working toward a long-term goal will provide you with the motivation and passion to take you through. Once you have identified your goal, motivation, and sometimes a little fear comes naturally. Sure, figuring out what you really want does take some time and you absolutely have to be willing to do the required introspective work. The beauty is, once the work is done you will find the answer is crystal clear, obstacles seem to become only slight irritations and the path becomes crystal clear. Though you may fear the leap beyond what you know, the journey will yield many rewards. And it sure beats the alternative!

## Take Responsibility for Your Choices

We all like to have someone else to blame for our
disappointments. "If my boss had treated me more
fairly . . ." "If my parents had saved enough money to send
me to college . . ." These little resentments build up like acid
with no place to go. And guess who is the container for the
acid. That's right—YOU! You can hold it, but it gradually
eats away at you. Sure, you may splash a little bit of it on
somebody else once in awhile, but in the end, *you* are the
one who suffers.

When you keep in mind that the person you are today
is a cumulative result of all of your experiences it becomes
apparent how each situation was valuable. It is never too
late to regroup! If you aren't spending the majority of your
time in the positive zone, take the challenge to look inward
today! *You* will be the main benefactor of the terrific results!

# Stress—It Can Be A Good Thing!

*"Small minds are much distressed
by little things.
Great minds see them all but are not
upset by them."*

— *Francois de La Rochefoucauld*

You wake up after a fitful night of sleep, travel for 45 minutes in a dangerous environment with hostile strangers around you, and get bombarded with unfamiliar information. Sound like you are in a foxhole during wartime? Nah ... that describes how many of us feel just driving to work every day. In today's environment, we are subjected to so much stress that we often feel overwhelmed. By all accounts, we are simply not wired to handle so much pressure. We hang on, thinking that "soon", things will slow down. Forgeddaboutit. If anything, the pace will pick up. How can you use this fact to succeed in today's environment, rather than become overwhelmed by it?

## Take Control of Your Time

Time is absolutely, positively our most valuable commodity. It is the one thing that does not increase in supply in relation to the demand. Once it's gone, it's gone forever. The trick is to consistently schedule yourself for balance and efficiency. My commute time was previously a dreaded portion of each day. Now, I use this time to return calls on my hands-free cell phone, look at nature through my sunroof and listen to books on tape, and my commute is a breeze. If I am in a traffic jam, I call ahead to inform the person I am meeting of my delay and simply retreat to my "personal learning space."

## Deal with What *Actually* Happens

One of the most valuable traits we can develop is the one that allows us to heed our inner voice. I've said it before, I'll say it again: the largest percent of things we worry about never actually happen. While it sounds simple to focus on what actually *does* happen and then take action on the things we can control, most of us waste time imagining what coulda', shoulda', woulda' happened. Try handling just the situation at hand and you will find that you have the skills you need to make it through anything. Rely on your track record for being a survivor and having the ability to come up with creative solutions.

## Be Selective with Your Activities

I used to be addicted to the daily newspaper. I literally could not go to sleep at night without reading it. Now, I compromise by listening to both local and international news while getting ready for work and reading the local weekly business newspaper. With the prevalence of online newspapers, we can read summaries and take in the highlights within a few minutes, rather than spend hours trying to take in the vast amounts of information available to us. By omitting habits and activities that are time-wasters, we can come up with "found" time to reorganize. How often do you go somewhere or do something just to please someone else? Try coming up with one extra hour per week and you may soon find that you become adept at reorganizing available minutes.

## Start Fresh Each Day

Do you keep a perpetual "To Do List"? At the end of the day, does the list consist of as many "left-over" tasks as completed ones? Beginning each day with uncompleted tasks can be demoralizing and create the stressful feeling that you *never* have enough time to finish anything. Try making several lists. Your Daily List would be made up of items absolutely slated for completion on a given day. Your second list would contain "B" and "C" priorities added in as your time allows. At the end of each day, construct your Task List for the coming day. Add items from the lower priority list as your time allows. One of my clients keeps his completed lists in a file folder and refers to it for a reminder of his weekly accomplishments.

## Start Writing

The age-old art of writing has been somewhat lost in the age of computers. One terrific means of letting go of stress is to simply write about situations without holding back. We tend to hold discussions in our head when we are angry or frustrated, particularly with work situations, for fear of reprisal. By writing it out and saying exactly what is on your mind, you can release it and make more room in your head. One successful IT professional I know vents his frustrations and complaints in a *red* spiral notebook. He has a reputation as a terrific project manager, as he always maintains a calm and level head at work. He attributes this to his Red Venting Notebook, which gives him a means to empty angry, frustrated thoughts, and makes more room for productive ones.

# Start Moving

Mental stress creates quite a few physiological reactions. More organizations are recognizing this and offering Nap Rooms, on-site chair massages and gym memberships. When you get to the point that you are overwhelmed with priorities, take a break and do some physical exercise. Twenty minutes of physical activity will revitalize you. If at all possible, get outside where the sunlight or fresh air can help reenergize you. Walk rapidly up flights of stairs to get your blood flowing, do a few stretches, and above all, *breathe*. When we are stressed, we tend to breathe much shallower — or not at all — and the physical impact is obvious. A quick break will make a huge difference in your stamina.

Remember that stress provides adrenaline and can be a great motivator. It can present opportunities to excel or fail. Put these techniques into motion, and remember that we cannot control events, but we *can* control how we *react* — and that makes a world of difference.

# Top Ten Stress Busters

1. **Start moving** — Get a change of scenery . . . it revs up your blood flow, adjusts your focus and rejuvenates your tired muscles.
2. **Do "crazy brainstorming"** — Come up with 15-20 potential solutions to a current challenge . . . no matter how impractical. It reminds you that you *do* have choices!
3. **Stick to the facts** — Address only what has actually occurred and avoid spending time needlessly worrying about what *could* happen.
4. **Laugh** — A study tracked kids as laughing an average of 247 times a day, in contrast to adults laughing seven times. Look at the light side of situations!
5. **Vent** — Remember that it is OK to be upset about something. Vent about it and move on . . . keeping it inside will just zap energy.
6. **Start with a fresh task list each day** — Carrying over your list from day to day creates the impression that you will never finish . . . re-prioritize daily.
7. **Change gears** — When overwhelmed by a situation, put it aside and tackle something less challenging . . . coming back later presents a fresh perspective.
8. **Use potentially stressful times for catch-up activities** — Keep items in your car or briefcase to read or write when forced to wait . . . the time will fly by and you won't be stressing over the delay.
9. **Write about it** — Start a confidential Stress Journal and spend at least five minutes a day writing about

everything getting on your last nerve. You will
miraculously forget about most of it.

10. **Schedule rewards** — Even at the busiest times,
    schedule time for activities you consider to be fun . . .
    the balance will pay off in untold ways.

# CHAPTER FIVE

## Communicating to Get What You Want

# Winning Communication Strategies

---

*"Good communication is just as stimulating*
*as black coffee, and just*
*as hard to sleep after."*

— *Anne Morrow Lindbergh*

---

With slang becoming more prevalent, I suggest that it is time to go back to using a more gracious, direct communication style. You know, John Wayne, Aunt Bea, The Godfather and Mae West, all rolled into one. That is, we need to be more adept at really *connecting* to others. The high tech world rules, and this means that we humans are spending more and more time alone. I recently read about a study concurring that the number one thing humans crave is intimacy — any type of open, honest human contact.

With the increased use of voice mail, e-mail and slang, there is a lot of room for misinterpretation. Following are a few guidelines to make your communication more powerful.

## Two-Way Street

Communication is a two-way street — meaning that we are supposed to be talking and listening. When one party dominates the discussion, the other party tunes out very quickly. Think about the last time you listened to someone at a lectern or pulpit. Exactly how long did it take you to drift off into your own side scenario? Involvement of both parties makes all the difference. In a gospel church service, where people speak out whenever they feel like it ("Amen, sister" . . . "Oh, yes" . . . "I hear ya" . . . "That's right"), everyone in the audience is in the conversation. Don't be a talking head! Get the other parties involved and effective communication will be the result.

## Tune In

Remember that no matter how brief a conversation, it will be more meaningful if you really tune in to the other party. Make eye contact and focus only on the person(s) with whom you are talking. Several years ago, I was in Washington, D.C. on Christmas Eve and happened upon Bill and Chelsea Clinton out shopping. I reached out to shake Clinton's hand and will never forget the experience — eyes locked; strong, two-handed shake; and a warmth, energy and charisma that would impact anyone. (In retrospect, I don't think it was just the beret I was wearing.) His ability to make a person feel as though he or she is the only one around is what makes him magnetic. When talking with others, really tune in to them — even if it is just for 30 seconds — and you may be amazed by the improvement in your communication.

## Be Appropriate

A good rule of thumb when at work or in casual conversation is to keep the topics to work, world of finance, recreation/sports, family/friends and general news. By following this guideline, you will avoid offending others or stepping into sensitive areas. I recently attended a business seminar and during a break, engaged in conversation with a woman in the class. Within five minutes, she began telling me about her five plastic surgery procedures, methods, results, cost, level of pain and then . . . no kidding . . . pulled "before and after" pictures out of her purse. Needless to say, this person did not impress me as someone with whom I want to do business.

## Communication = 55% Body, 38% Tone, 7% Words

Were you aware that the words we speak are the **smallest** percent of what makes up communication? Our body language and voice tone make up 93% of our communication. If this seems incredible, think about all the stories you hear about people "falling in love" on the Internet. They are only communicating with words—7% of the communication. Of course, this results in *lots* of room for using one's imagination and misunderstanding the other party. Being aware of your body language and your tone, and the huge impact they have on the other party results in more understanding of what someone truly meant and less what you think they might have meant.

### Ask for What You Want

"You don't ask, you don't get" . . . a phrase perhaps overused, but so true. We often are hesitant to ask for what we really need for fear of appearing self-centered. Unless you consistently ask for things to the detriment of others, asking for what you want or need is right on target—the other party can't just read your mind. While there appear to be some gifted psychics out there, I find that being direct often results in getting exactly what you need and desire. Approach others in an open-ended manner, such as "What would it take to change our meeting from today to Friday?" This lets them know that you are open to compromise. **"The Aladdin Factor"** by Jack Canfield and Mark Victor Hansen is a wonderful source of success stories resulting from coming out and letting the other party know what is desired.

## Be Credible

We all know people who exaggerate, always forget the punch line and can never name a source. Then there are the name-droppers who attempt to impress simply by association. Knowing the facts and always being able to back up what you say will build you a reputation for credibility. Remember to focus on your own accomplishments — they are more important than any you could invent.

These guidelines will keep your communication open, honest and interesting. Remember, once something is said, you can't take it back. So if you are really at a loss for words, ask the other party lots of questions and let them do the talking!

# Making Your Best First Impression

---

*"In a world where first impressions
are everything —
You have to make sure you get it right
the first time."*

*— Unknown*

---

$T$ ake a look in the mirror. Be brave — make it a full-length one. What would *you* think if *you* saw *you* walking down the street? First impressions are made instantly and are quite difficult to change. After someone has given you the once-over, you have to work hard to turn that opinion around. Always give a topnotch first impression and you'll come out a winner, no matter *what* the situation!

## The Most Important Rule—Be Real

The "product" you offer to the world or sell to a potential employer is who you *truly* are . . . all the time. If you simply *create* a role to please others, you can never be fully comfortable in that role. Of course, the biggest obstacle when putting on a false front is the chance that you may forget what it is! Strive to improve yourself in every way, but be proud of who you are in any role. Your "can do" attitude will shine through.

*"No one can make you feel inferior without
your consent."*

**— Eleanor Roosevelt**

The whole idea of making a terrific first impression is to
*be comfortable* in your own skin. Decide what image you
want to present; then do the most with how to live that
image! We can all reinvent ourselves—just invest the time
and energy!

Here are a few ideas to consider:

- **Research your destination in advance.** For example,
  before attending a professional organization for the
  first time, find out about the mission, officers or
  speaker's topic. If you are headed to an interview,
  check out the company's Web site to get a flavor for
  their culture. We all feel more confident when we
  are informed about a subject. Think of a few topics
  you can talk about with others.
- **Dress the part you want to play.** If you want to be
  in management, wear a jacket with your business
  casual outfits. Purchase one terrific suit and make
  sure you have it tailored to fit. Nothing looks worse
  than cuffs that are too long on an otherwise dynamite
  jacket.

  Your shoes are just as important. They don't have
  to be new, just well maintained. Worn-down or
  unpolished shoes send a strong, unfavorable message.
- **Wear classic accessories.** I recommend basic colors
  for accessories, such as brown, black or tan. That way,
  your briefcase will always look terrific. Your
  wristwatch or other jewelry can make or break your
  polished look. Keep them simple—leave the sparkly
  stuff for nighttime. Avoid noisy dangle bracelets,

necklaces or earrings. Leave the political buttons and tongue rings at home as well.

- **Project a positive attitude.** This is so easy to manage and absolutely, positively 100% within your control. It is tough to fake a positive attitude or enthusiastic opinion. Write a positive script and use some self-talk on the way to your event.

  Some years ago, I had a habit of worrying about the "what ifs" on the way to important events. For example, *"What if they ask me a question I don't know how to answer? "What if I forget someone's name when doing introductions? "What if I have spinach in my teeth and no one tells me."*

  I finally made the *choice* to take a 180-degree turn and programmed a positive outcome. The result should be more like this: *"I am going to have a great time at the meeting. I will be connecting with interesting people with whom I enjoy discussing business. The contacts I make will be mutually beneficial."*

- **Make direct eye contact.** This is one of the most important components of making a favorable first impression. Look directly into the other person's eyes—or from person to person if you're meeting a group. Take time to connect and nod.

- **Smile.** This one is so simple that it is often overlooked altogether. Sit in a lobby and just watch how many people are smiling. Still looking for one? At any rate, it is the one equalizer we can all use in any setting anywhere in the world. Smile! What are you afraid of? Someone won't smile back? So what? Don't be afraid to break the ice—set the tone with a terrific smile.

- **Give a strong handshake with your right hand** and make eye contact as you shake. It speaks volumes about your confidence and energy level. Don't grab the person's hand with both of your hands. Shake three to four times and let go . . . don't be the lounge lizard who hangs on to the other person's hand way too long. And avoid touching the other person's shoulder, elbow or whatever, unless you already know them quite well.

If you are nervous about sweaty palms, stop to wash and dry your hands right before going into the meeting or event. Wipe your palms with one of those moist towelettes. This will dry your palms. You can also try using talcum powder (sparingly) on your palms.

- **Repeat the person's name to yourself as they are introduced** and try to remember one small detail that does not change—eye color, teeth, height. This will help you to connect them to their name the next time you meet.

- **Take in the surroundings** and try to assimilate to the atmosphere. If the tone is quiet, let others take the lead. Observe and make every effort to fit in, rather than draw attention to yourself in an effort to stand out. You will avoid the *wrong* kind of attention!

Tune in to others, smile, make eye contact and be real. Keep a low profile as you build your comfort level in a new situation. You'll make a great impression, whether you are at a wrestling match or meeting the queen!

# The Art Of Asking

---

*"It is a funny thing about life; if you refuse to accept anything but the best, you very often get it."*

— *Somerset Maughm*

---

Learning *how* to ask for what you really want and need is one of the most basic ways to meet your needs. And yet, when did you last ask for something? Most of us unreasonably expect others to know what we need by reading our minds. Then when our needs are not met, we complain and act like a victim. We may be victimized by the ego that cannot ask for help — or the low self-esteem that assumes we are not worthy of it. You must break the vicious cycle of being afraid to ask! Learn to perfect your asking techniques.

One of my all-time favorite television characters is Colombo. In his show, he follows his suspects around, coming up with just one more question. The one question to get just enough information to solve the mystery. If you employ this method in your own life, you can enjoy the same result.

When I was growing up, my father often said, "You don't ask, you don't get." It seemed brash and rude, and nothing could make me ask. As the years went by, there were hundreds of occasions where I chose not to ask for anything. While I had always made it through life just fine, I have since learned to make my life easier by knowing what I want and learning to ask for it. The biggest lesson I learned was that humans are helpful and want to be of service.

## Why Do We Hesitate to Ask?

- **F.E.A.R.** — "False Expectations Appearing Real." Little tapes play in our heads, such as, "If I ask, I will look weak"; "If I ask, they might say 'no'"; or "If I ask, I will owe them something." Blah, blah, blah. Most of these fears are totally unfounded. The truth is that most people like to help.
- "I don't deserve it" is another big reason is that we hesitate to ask. Everyone learned the tapes about being selfish. You know, "If you ask for something for yourself, that is selfish. Do what is right for the group." While there is truth in this, taking care of yourself is the key to helping others.
- **On some level, we *like* being victims.** When our needs are not met, we can moan and groan about how others don't understand us; we are givers and everyone else is a taker. Try writing a mental prescription for a positive outcome. Part of asking is believing that the outcome will be decided in your favor. And even if it is not, at least you tried. Now a new decision tree opens. Does not getting this mean you will be unhappy? What steps can you take to remedy this? Either way, choosing to be a victim is just that — a choice. What would you think of someone who chose to be a victim?
- **We are too proud to ask.** The American way is one of self-sufficiency and the ability to earn your way

from the ground up. We once knew a sense of community where everyone helped their fellow residents. As life grew more complicated and competitive, asking for help became a blow to our ego.

- **We simply don't know what we want.** We can't clarify our wishes to ourselves, which makes it impossible to enlist the help of others. We are great at knowing what we *don't* want, so we end up spending too much time turning down offers of help from others. Perhaps the time would be best spent exploring options that may lead us, perhaps though the elimination of alternatives, to what we do want most for ourselves.

## Life Is A Buffet

Have you ever dined at an all you-can-eat buffet? Compare your approach to this experience with the way you view life.

- **Do you have the abundance mentality?** This is the view that there is plenty of food up there and you want to try it all. You want to get your money's worth.
- **Do you view the buffet as having so many choices that you can't possibly figure out what to select?** You are overwhelmed just looking at it and avoid making new choices, so you select what is familiar to you. While this is comfortable, you may be missing delights that you have no idea exist.
- **Do you have a scarcity mentality?** This is the feeling that you had better get up there fast to get your share. All of the good stuff will no doubt be gone soon and never be replenished. You might even carry some plastic baggies in your pocket to take food home.

*Camille M. Primm*

# The Helicopter Ride

While traveling across country, I planned a stop at the Grand Canyon. I was even going to spring for a helicopter ride. A friend had told me about his experience and said he hoped I got the front seat, as the view was far more spectacular. When I arrived at the canyon and purchased my ticket, I joined numerous others waiting for their flights.

Spotting a person near the 'copter, I walked over and asked what it would take to ride up front with the pilot. I was told it was based on weight balance, but the person asked my name. I'm sure you have already figured out that I grinned from ear to ear as I jumped into the seat they assigned . . . right next to the pilot . . . and the ride was breathtaking! When we disembarked, several of my fellow passengers asked me how I got to ride up front. "I asked", was my response.

Take *your* seat at the buffet of life. Ask for what you need and want—and your life will take on a completely different tone. Ask and you will get!

# Small Talk Made Simple

---

*"The most important thing in communication
is hearing what isn't said."*

*— Peter F. Drucker*

---

The process of learning to speak as toddlers is one of the most exciting things we can experience. Finally, we can communicate to others . . . let them know what we want, let them know how much we appreciate them (right!) and explain what's on our mind. Talking is not only second nature, it represents a universal means of communicating.

If talking is so common . . . and literally second nature . . . then why do some of us break out in a cold sweat at the idea of going to an event where we don't know anyone? Why is making conversation a dreaded activity for a big portion of the population?

## Does Small Talk Make You Clam Up?

When you go to a business meeting or conference, are you psyched at the possibility of meeting new people? Do you effortlessly glide into a room where you don't know a SOUL and sidle right up to a stranger to begin chatting? When you have to carpool to a training class with a coworker you don't know very well, do your hands get clammy as you count the minutes of silence? Well, no more . . . learn to master the art of small talk.

# Make a Great First Impression!

The art of making small talk is a breeze when you learn a few techniques. You don't have to be an extrovert to feel comfortable in *any* social situation.

A first impression is made instantaneously, so use this fact to your advantage. Before heading to an event, pay attention to your grooming. Stand in front of a full-length mirror—would *you* want to talk to *you*? Are your clothes clean, well fitting and pressed? Little things like neatly styled hair, clean hands and nails, shined shoes and a freshly scrubbed look never go out of style!

## Picture Successful Interactions

On the way to the event, take time to picture a successful outcome. Let your thoughts flow in a positive manner. Imagine yourself meeting individuals who share your interests and are anxious to talk with you. Take deep breaths and "see" yourself easily talking with people. Visualize smooth conversation. The subconscious can't distinguish between reality and imagination, so why not set yourself up for success?

Above all, be "real". Putting on airs or being someone you aren't, in an effort to impress others, will result in confusion, not only for yourself, but for them as well. And you'll grow tired of acting rather quickly because you'll have to remember exactly what you've told to whom!

## Joining a Conversation

When you enter a room and people are already milling about, talking in small groups, look around and find a group of three or more people. Avoid groups of two, as they may be having a private discussion. When you walk up to the group, be aware of how close you stand. Give others their personal space, but stand near enough to be included. Smile and say hello, or nod. When they stop their discussion, introduce yourself and offer your hand to shake theirs. Tune in and make an effort to learn by carefully listening to their discussion.

## Socially Acceptable Topics

A common mistake is bringing up offensive topics or subjects that raise strong feelings in others. If you start a conversation by poking fun at someone's hairpiece, you may be talking to a person who wears one as well!

You have no doubt heard that you should avoid talking about sex, politics and religion. What's left, you ask? There are countless topics of a benign nature that can be interesting and create hours of discussion. A few of the most common are:

- Travel
- High Profile Personalities
- Current Events
- Recreation
- Entertainment
- Friends
- Family
- Cars
- Sports

To remain current on any of these topics, pick up a newspaper or magazine, or flip on the TV to get a few tidbits of information.

## Be an Incredible Listener

One of the biggest success strategies in conversation is being a fantastic listener. The ability to ask questions and really *tune in* to answers is a rare talent. If you take time to pay attention and really care about the other person's opinions and ideas, it will be noticed immediately.

Jacqueline Kennedy Onassis was a well-known listener. Noted for paying rapt attention to the other party, she genuinely tuned in and asked questions to encourage more conversation. She made a great impression and charmed many, not by talking a blue streak, but by her ability to listen and make the other person feel important. This technique works wonders for introverts.

So there you have it. You, too, can be a sparkling conversationalist by just tuning in, asking questions, being interested and showing up for others. When you put the spotlight on others, you will surely be remembered as a fascinating person!

# Understanding Basic Communication Styles

---

*"No one would talk much in society,
if he only knew how often he misunderstands
others."*

*— Goethe*

---

Everyone has experienced meeting someone with whom they felt either instantly comfortable or disliked for no apparent reason. Every day, we face the challenge of being understood and accurately interpreting others. We are actually more likely to misinterpret something we hear or read than to correctly decipher every nuance in a discussion.

Numerous organizational psychologists have studied personality types and how differences impact communication. The work of one noted Swiss researcher, Dr. Carl Jung, was developed by Drake Beam Morin into a widely used assessment tool — I-Speak Your Language®. The instrument has applications for both business and personal situations and is quite uncomplicated. Tuning in to another person's style allows us to adapt our own approach to better connect with the other party.

# The Four Basic Styles

The I-Speak® process places personalities into four basic categories. I have rarely seen participants complete the assessment and experience a huge awakening. Rather, it gives a common language to the styles. I have often heard the comment that it would be a good idea to have couples complete the assessment before being granted a marriage license!

Look at the table below and determine which style is most like yours:

| Style | Typical Traits | Time Orientation | Behavioral | |
|---|---|---|---|---|
| | | | Pros | Cons |
| **Feeler** | Places a high value on how situations impact people. Skilled at "reading between the lines" and assembling terrific teams. | Past | Empathetic Persuasive Spontaneous Loyal

Traditional | Too personal Manipulative Impulsive Plays Favorites

Sentimental |
| **Intuitor** | Values ideas, future thinking and innovation. Creative and skilled at long-range planning. Great at creating a vision for the future. | Future | Idealistic Ideological Creative

Original Imaginative | Unrealistic Impractical Fantasy-bound

Out of touch Too far out |
| **Thinker** | Places value on statistics, logic and precise procedures. They can maintain projects and maximize profits by checking out all the details. | Past Present Future | Prudent Objective Rational Analytical Deliberative | Over-cautious Controlling Rigid Too serious Indecisive |
| **Sensor** | Values implementation and action. They are the drivers who have the skill to translate plans into profits. Successful at getting projects off the ground and covering all bases. | Present | Perfectionist Wants results Objective Decisive Pragmatic | Nit-picker Status-seeker Act, then think Self-involved Shortsighted |

By now, you have probably identified your own style by reading through the above table. While we occasionally exhibit traits from each of the four styles, we default to our predominant style under normal circumstances. So what can you do with this knowledge?

## Tune In to Others!

The purpose of communication is to exchange information, build relationships and understand others, right? Understanding where the other party is coming from will give you the advantage of being able to take steps to adjust your *own* style to better match *theirs*.

## Keys for Each Type

Here is a quick list of each type, along with thoughts on the best way to appeal to their style:

- **Feelers** are quite tuned in to the emotions and reactions of others. Let them know how you *feel* about things. They most likely have memorabilia, such as awards, photos or trophies, displayed around their office. Take a look and comment. You might have something in common, such as your golf handicap.
- **Intuitors** are very idea-oriented, always thinking of the future and possibilities. They typically overlook the people side of a situation, focusing instead on the big picture. Their surroundings are often messy, and contain abstract art and multiple resources, such as books and magazines. Reach them by coming up with a different way to approach something or suggesting an unusual twist.
- **Thinkers** go strictly by the book. They are very factual, calm, unemotional and systematic. Their surroundings are neat and minimal, often with charts and graphs on the wall. Get a Thinker's attention by supporting your

ideas with facts. Look for things that may go wrong and come up with options in advance. Create step-by-step procedures.

- **Sensors** are the doers—the ones who can probably be reached by cell phone, pager, shoe phone, or whatever. They are action-oriented and want results *now*. Typically, they expect people to do "whatever it takes to get the job done" and overlook minor details like a "life". Their workspace is cluttered with a look of disorganization. The Sensor feels comfortable when you avoid going into too much detail and show an interest in getting things rolling *now*.

This information can make a dramatic difference in how people perceive you and how successful you are in your relationships with others. Remember, there is *no one style* that is better than another. Each has advantages and weaknesses. A combination of *all* styles creates dynamic teams and incredible results. *Tune in* and watch your frustration level with others diminish in no time!

# Business Communication
# Tips For Women

---

*"The articulate voice is more distracting than mere noise."*

*— Seneca*

---

The gender landscape is finally shifting. The revered and powerful "Good Old Boys' Network" is slowly being given a face-lift to allow for the increasing number of women in business today.

The interesting thing is that the "Good Old Boys' Network" perpetuated itself by men of one generation helping the next one along. Having a "godfather" in the business meant that you had a much higher chance of success because you had someone to pull strings for you.

My observation is that the "Girls' Network" thrives on an entirely different principle. I see women mentoring each another to ensure that they have a chance to learn the ropes. Many women in the work force grew up without role models or learning competition through sports. They pass on information partially due to their natural inclination to nurture.

# Business Obstacles

In her work *"Woman to Woman"*, author Judith Briles conducted a recent study that surveyed women in the workplace. When asked what barriers they faced in their careers, four key obstacles were cited: prejudice, communication, sabotage and poor management.

- Prejudice includes discrimination based upon age, looks, sex and race. While this is a gray area, our perception is the reality from which we operate. As victims of alleged discrimination, women and their ultimate success are adversely affected.
- Communication is the "make or break" skill for any businessperson, but women should be particularly aware of the image they present and the message they send to others.
- Sabotage was listed as a problem by 71% of the women surveyed in the 1994 *"Briles Report"*. They stated that they had been undermined and sabotaged by female coworkers.
- Management trap means supervision as in too much, too little, the wrong mentors, or the lack thereof. Lots of individuals in the workplace have been promoted beyond their level of competency. Many women reported being interrupted when talking, criticized when they disagreed with their manger, and sometimes called emotional. In addition, many stated that their title might indicate a level of authority but they often were not given the authority it warranted.

## Success Strategy

These key obstacles really bring home the message that

women must continue to develop their communication skills to remain competitive. Try these proven tips to help you succeed, regardless of your profession or position:

## Use Assertive Mannerisms

- Good eye contact will ensure that others take you more seriously.
- Lack of strong eye contact can mean submissiveness, fear and nervousness.
- Women are more apt to use direct eye contact, so use it to your advantage.

## Smiling

- Women tend to smile more and inappropriately, especially during conflict.
- Worse, women may giggle when nervous.
- Use your smile to project confidence and sincerity.

## Head Nodding Up and Down

- Men typically nod to symbolize that they agree with what is being said.
- Women nod just to indicate that they are taking in information.
- Avoid nodding to a male coworker when you are just listening and not agreeing.

## Learn to Sell Yourself

- Make business a common topic in your social communication.
- Showcase your knowledge.
- Make others aware of your skills.

## Speak with Conviction

- Remember, self-confidence is the number one requirement for a leader.
- Don't allow yourself to be interrupted when talking.

## Tell It Like It Is

- Don't sugarcoat your comments or feedback.
- Give only direct and honest constructive criticism.

## Be Logical in Your Communication

- Use facts and data to support your opinions.
- Avoid limiting your credibility by using such phrases as I "feel" and say I "think" or "know".
- Apply goal-oriented language.
- State the facts and avoid a lot of unnecessary storytelling.

Women have unlimited opportunities in today's business climate. Communication skills are one of the biggest factors impacting success or mediocrity in your career. Act confident, though you may not really feel it and genuine confidence will follow. Remember, we are what we perceive. If we project confidence, others perceive it and we are apt to see ourselves through their eyes. Be assertive and your confidence will soar in every situation!

# Men Vs. Women In Communication

---

*"Men and women belong to different species
and communications between
them is still in its infancy."*

— *Bill Cosby*

---

$W$e all have different styles of communication, developed by various influences, including our:

- Economic, cultural and geographical environments
- Educational background
- Personal experiences
- Age
- Gender

While no one style is better than another, men and women generally talk differently with varying degrees of male/female speech characteristics. The styles have been described as "relate vs. debate", "competitive vs. cooperative" and "report vs. rapport".

- Men generally go for the straightforward solution to a problem. They tend to come up with advice.
- Women try to build relationships by discussing problems. They show empathy but don't give advice unless asked.

Understanding gender differences in business communication creates a more productive workplace, definitely builds rapport and helps avoid costly misinterpretations.

## Logic vs. Intuition

When communicating, the split between "male logic" and "female intuition" is a debate as old as language itself. Since men and women are motivated by different factors and have different needs, they simply do not understand each other. It's not about being "equal" — men and women just choose different ways to process and convey information.
Generally speaking, we find the following to be true:

- Women use language to create intimacy and build rapport with others; they converse.
- Men use language to negotiate and maintain their status and independence; they talk.

## Key Differences

There are a number of great books that assess the differences in communication styles based upon gender and personal relationships. Tuning in to these differences can reinforce successful business relationships, regardless of gender. Following are some of the most widely recognized differences:

- **Body language** — Men and women give off different nonverbal signals. For instance, men generally nod during a conversation to indicate, "I agree with you", while women nod to indicate, "I understand what you are saying".
- **Sensitivity to nonverbal language of others** is shown considerably more by women than men. Men also provide fewer facial expressions.

- **Both like power** — Generally speaking, men seek it and women accept it. Women assume power when it is granted.

- **Playing down one's own power** is a female characteristic. Women are more likely to be empathetic when coworkers have problems. Men jump in and offer solutions.

- **Accepting criticism** — Women personalize criticism more than men.

- **The use of polite speech** shows a high regard for others. However, there are times when extremely polite speech lacks necessary business assertiveness. Women are apt to use "tag" phrases such as", If you are OK with that", whereas men simply state their opinion.

- **Decisions are made quicker** by men than by women. Females have a tendency to get input and build a consensus before rendering a decision. Men typically avoid consulting with others and make singular decisions.

- **Bragging and playing up accomplishments** is more routinely a male dominant behavior. Since men frequently take vocal credit for their accomplishments, they are commonly awarded with promotions or bonuses based upon such declaration. Women are now beginning to use similar strategies for immediate gratification.

- **Interruptions during conversation** are tolerated and accepted more readily by women than by men. And men are usually the ones interrupting!

- **Asking for help** is one of the oldies. Women are more likely to ask for and accept help than men. Some experts believe this trait can enhance their management skills.

- **Asking questions** takes more time for men than for women. Men give more pre-questions and details. Women tend to ask multiple questions at one time.

- **Assertive behavior** is viewed by both sexes as positive. Studies show that assertive behavior by females appraised equally with that of males.
- **Personal issues** are much more likely to be brought up for discussion by women than men. Men generally limit their dialogue to business and current events.
- **"Telling it like it is"** is probably expressed more frequently by men than women. Men give direct feedback, while women may soften it by first stating what the person did *right*.

The more aware you are to gender differences in communication styles, the more successful you will be in your own communication . . . and in *all* aspects of your life!

# Interpreting Body Language

---

*"When the eyes say one thing, and the tongue
another, a practiced man relies
on the language of the first."*

— Emerson

---

Body language, or the science of *kinesthetics*, is a fascinating subject that few people ever study. We study foreign languages but often overlook learning how to interpret the nonverbal language that is so critical to our daily communication.

## Components of Communication

Albert Mehrabian (*"Nonverbal Communication,"* Chicago: Aldine-Atherton, 1972) found through his research that communication is based on 55% nonverbal signals, 38% tone of voice, and a mere 7% actual words. While most realize the significance of gestures, we too often misinterpret or entirely ignore them because we never learned how to read them.

Research confirms that the old saying, "Actions speak louder than words", has a lot of merit. When verbal and nonverbal language is inconsistent, we tend to believe the nonverbal. It is definitely harder to fake.

# Common Cues

Being able to expertly read a person's body language requires extensive training and experience. But let's take a look at some of the most common gestures to help increase your awareness of what others are saying in their nonverbal conversational actions:

- **Smiling and frowning:** These are the only universal gestures readily understood by everyone.
- **Cocking the head:** Charles Darwin noticed early in his studies that animals, as well as humans, tend to cock their heads slightly whenever they hear something that interests them. It gives the impression of listening intently.
- **Touching the nose:** Usually performed with an index finger, this is a sign of rejection. The person probably does not agree with what is being said.
- **Rubbing the eye:** This is another sign of doubt.
- **Steepling the hands:** Whether hands are held high or low, this gesture shows confidence and power.
- **Clearing the throat:** Men tend to use this as a signal to correct one's behavior. It also indicates nervousness and apprehension.
- **Locking the ankles:** The person is holding something back, such as strong feelings. This is often accompanied by clenched hands.
- **Folding the arms across the chest:** The person is listening but is resisting or disagreeing with what the speaker is saying or doing.
- **Leaning toward another person:** This is a classic indication that a person is listening intently and wants the speaker to know it.
- **Holding the hand partially across the mouth while speaking:** This denotes a lack of self-confidence, uncertainty or anxiety.

- **Open body posture:** The most positive of all gestures—this suggests receptivity and willingness to listen.

## Observe Clusters of Cues

One reason we often misinterpret nonverbal language is that we look at it separately, rather than in clusters. For example, a person with crossed arms may simply be cold, not resistant.

You can better interpret nonverbal messages by looking at the entire image, rather than singular signs. For example, if you are animated, moving forward and smiling all at once, the other person can tell you are happy to see them.

## Matching Behavior

Mirroring someone's body language is a common communication technique defined in the study of Neuro-Linguistics (NLP). This is called "matching" and eases the conversation. Studies show that the larger the difference in body language, the less likely a conversation will flow easily. The speaker will "think" you are not connected, and in almost all instances, stop talking. Purposely matching the other person's behavior will make them feel comfortable so they are more likely to be open with you.

Once you begin tuning in to the major part of communication—the nonverbal element—you will see a vast improvement in correctly understanding others. *Pay close attention to body language—it rarely lies!*

# Techniques for Resolving Communication Differences

---

*"Whenever you're in **conflict** with someone,
there is one factor that can
make the difference between damaging your
relationship and deepening it.
That factor is attitude.*

— *William James*

---

Conflict is inevitable. Even though it is a basic part of communication, many of us are uncomfortable dealing with it. The more we avoid conflict, the less practice we get resolving it. Conflict simply represents the fact that our needs or the needs of others have not been met in some way. Or conflict indicates our interests or values have been challenged. The idea is to seek a mutually beneficial way to resolve conflicts as they occur. Here are my top five conflict resolution strategies:

- **Keep gender differences in mind.** Women, being nurturing by nature, are inclined to avoid confrontation. They tend to take it personally. Men tend to confront conflict directly and immediately.

They typically stay more focused on coming to resolution quickly.

- **Think as "We" instead of "You vs. Me"** and the tone is set for compromise. Hold discussions in a neutral area at a mutually beneficial time to eliminate the psychological home turf advantage.
- **Look for mutually beneficial resolutions** and both parties will end up coming out better than before the conflict began. When we walk away feeling cheated . . . or even like we always outsmart the other party, nobody wins.
- **Think of the long term.** If you keep the big picture in mind, the realization comes that the idea is to build long-term relationships. Things seem to come out even in the long run anyway. A big benefit is that everyone can approach situations with honesty when a solid relationship is involved and trust has been built.
- **Become known as a Mediator** by taking responsibility for confronting and resolving conflict when it arises. Take care of situations in a timely and mutually beneficial way and you will play a key role in creating a dynamic environment of communication.

The skill to resolve conflict is a valuable tool, as disagreements won't ever just fade away when ignored. If you embrace dissension as an opportunity, it will serve to build both better relationships **and** communication.

# Listen Up!

---

---

"I listen fine. It's the *others* who have a problem!" Ever known someone who just doesn't focus — doesn't quite hear what is being said? Was it ever *you*? Now is a good time to review your listening skills. If you are anything like I am, you never took a class called "How to Listen".

## Concentrate and Observe

Listening is defined as the ability to concentrate mentally and observe carefully. It is applying oneself to *hearing* something. Obviously, one must pay attention in order to listen effectively. And that's where we sometimes fall short.

Our diverse work environment requires terrific listening skills. Studies show that we spend about 80% of our waking hours communicating, and at least 45% of that time listening. Take a few moments to explore some skills that will hone your ability to listen up

# The Listening Process

Listening is a four-step process and skipping any one of them causes it to break down. The steps are:

- **Hear**—by simply paying attention to the speaker
- **Interpret**—by tuning in to body language
- **Evaluate**—what the speaker really means and what you will do with the info
- **Respond**—by asking questions

## Golden Nuggets for Good Listening

**Listen intellectually.** When we hear someone else talking, we instinctively begin to project our own experiences, opinions, biases and interpretations. We start processing before the other person has even expressed their thoughts. Concentrate on the speaker's *words* and watch their face for extra clues.

**Exploit your brainpower.** We think four times faster than we can speak! That is one reason we have so much time to project our own interpretations. Instead, try using the listening lag time to really tune in and actually repeat the speaker's words in your own head. Read their lips! This will ensure that you are hearing the words, rather than thinking of your reply.

**Make eye contact.** Have you ever observed others in a restaurant? I find that people who are really tuned in—such as couples in love—have their eyes locked on each other. They lean forward and the one listening nods in acknowledgment. People who just give "ear service", that is, hear, but not really *listen*, look around the room, leaning back in their seats.

In the world of wolves, the "Alpha" is the one in control. He uses eye contact to wield power over the rest of the pack. Face the speaker—you need to be able to catch every signal. Speakers work harder at sending out information when they see a receptive audience. Eye contact helps complete the communication process. Try it—you'll notice a difference!

**Listen actively.** Active listening involves not only eye contact, but also body language in general. In contrast to passive listening, you will be sending non-verbal responses. Nod the head when the speaker talks, lean forward and acknowledge them by saying things such as, "I see" and "Uh-huh". Smile! You get the picture. Let them know you are tuned in versus just hearing.

**Listen between the lines.** Is there an underlying message? Are they giving you enough details? Is anything keeping you from "getting" what they are trying to express? Store these key points in your head for later when the speaker stops to catch his/her breath. These points will be fodder for your responses.

**Ask questions!** With all the information you have gained, you now have an opportunity to clarify *before* you interpret. You have read between the lines, so ask for details to fill in the blanks. Rudyard Kipling wrote: *"I keep six honest serving men (They taught me all I knew); Their names are What and Why and When and How and Where and Who."*

**You don't have to be a great conversationalist—just be a great listener!** I learned at an early age to ask questions in situations where I didn't know anyone. For several years, I served as president of a world trade organization. During this time, I had the opportunity to host at meetings and conventions, which allowed me to meet quite a few dignitaries. I never worried about making small talk. I merely asked questions. Everyone loves to talk about themselves! Use this to your advantage and people will think you are fascinating after speaking with you. They will feel your effort to connect.

In self-assessment, only 5% rate themselves as superior or excellent listeners—be one of this minority and you will see an immediate improvement in your relationships.

# Top Ten Communication Tips

1. **Know Your Own Style and How to Adjust It** — Remember that there are many styles of communication and you need to adapt to the other party.
2. **Lock in on the Eye Contact** — It will help you connect with others, encourages confidence and increases credibility.
3. **Schedule Time for Important Discussions** — Make sure you do not delay or avoid addressing issues. Conversely, do not rush an important discussion if the time isn't right.
4. **Conversation is a Two-Way Street** — Remember to do as much listening as talking to ensure understanding.
5. **Project a Positive Image** — Smile, make eye contact and stay out of others' personal space.
6. **Ask for What You Need** — You will be much more likely to get it — be specific and be willing to give something back in return.
7. **Communication = 55% Body, 38% Tone, 7% Words** — Be aware of the impact of all three components and the "hidden" messages you may be sending.
8. **Practice Active Listening** — Check in with the other party by asking questions or rephrasing what they have said to ensure you are both on the same track.
9. **Be Credible** — Know your sources, and avoid name-dropping and the tendency to exaggerate.
10. **Follow up** — By doing what you say you are going to do — you will be known as reliable and credible.

# CHAPTER SIX

## Work Place Cultures

# International Business
# Customs And Protocol

---

*"It's a Small World After All"*

— *Walt Disney*

---

An interesting segment of my career was spent in the international business arena. Today, the entire world is within our reach in a nanosecond and many firms are interested in spreading their business network into foreign markets.

One reason firms may lack enthusiasm to break into foreign markets is that they have no idea how to develop business relationships overseas. Doing business internationally doesn't necessarily mean travel to exotic places. In reality, it may just consist of faxing correspondence or standing in a 3x6 trade show booth in a strange city, where you have no clue about the local people or customs.

While it is not a requirement to understand the culture or language of suppliers or customers, it will immeasurably enhance the relationship both between yourself and those you will deal with as potential customers abroad. Your career will be much more dynamic if you are able to relate to others — regardless of their origin. You will also be a natural fit for entertaining foreign guests, representing the firm at conferences and leading a global work force.

Possessing international business expertise will always give you a leg up on the competition. The following are a few basics to consider:

## Language

The United States is one of the few countries where a second language is not studied extensively in school. So, English is pretty much spoken everywhere you go. Translators are also readily available and can provide valuable cultural insights. However, anyone is pleased to see that a visitor has taken the time to learn a couple of phrases in their language.

Remember to speak more slowly in a multinational environment. And avoid using slang—there can be too many variables in the translation, causing miscommunication. One of the more notorious slip-ups was a slogan used by Braniff Airlines: "Travel on Leather". Translated into Spanish, the word for leather (Cuero) also means "naked". The resulting message, "Travel Naked", created quite a stir!

## Introductions

Americans are much less formal than most other cultures. When meeting others, we assume that we can quickly advance to a first-name basis. Instead, you should address people as Mr., Ms., or by their title, if you know it. Titles are also much more highly regarded in most countries. For example, in Germany, you would address an individual as "Herr Doktor" (Mr. Doctor) in a business setting, until the person invites you to address them more informally.

## Business Relationships

The *Wall Street Journal* highlights protocol as one of the most significant skills in demand. Other nationalities value the importance of taking time to build a personal relationship much more highly than Americans do. We often extend casual invitations without necessarily intending to follow through. When traveling domestically, I often hear, "Why don't you come by and visit sometime?" I doubt if some of those folks really want me to come by. In contrast, in other countries, my experience has been that the person making an invitation sincerely means it.

When entering into a new business relationship, take the time to really know the person. Ask about their background, experiences and family. Invite them to share lunch or dinner with you. Above all, do not try to close a business deal until you have established a comfort level.

One of the biggest mistakes Americans make is pressing for the deal before spending enough time to build rapport. Front-loading the relationship with time and genuine interest will pay off in the long run.

## The Business Card

The traditional European or Asian business card includes titles and shows more formality than an American business card. Often, a brief description about the product or translated information is on the reverse side of the card.

There is typically a high interest level in presenting the card with formality, reading it and making eye contact with the person. If you take someone's card and carelessly place it in your pocket without reading and acknowledging it, the other person may be insulted.

Begin your new global business relationships with a large dose of patience and genuine interest. Pay attention to formalities and make an attempt to learn something about the culture and language up-front. Your knowledge of international business protocol will set you apart from the crowd!

# A Diverse Employee Base: Every Company's Most Powerful Resource

---

*"Diversity is the one true thing we all have in common. Celebrate it every day."*

*— Unknown*

---

No matter how creative companies get in their attempts to attract new talent, the competition is still tough. Fact is, even when Human Resources is successful at bringing in candidates, or recruiters reach out to locate qualified applicants, some managers are still not equipped to select the best team. Few organizations invest in training their managers to properly interview, so some great talent inevitably slips through the cracks.

Setting the tone with a company's culture and atmosphere is a key factor in attracting the right mix of talent. When a potential candidate is brought in for an interview, they've already passed the hurdles of offering the needed skill base and experience. The interview process determines whether or not the candidate is credible, and bottom line, has the right personality to be a good fit.

Because it's human nature to gravitate toward people *most like ourselves*, an interviewer may fall into the trap of hiring associates who are essentially like them.

## Variety Builds New Ideas

University studies have proven the value of a diverse team. With the current blend of baby boomers and Gen-Xers in the workplace, it is even more apparent that a mixture of ideas and backgrounds builds a more dynamic and efficient workplace. In addition, the more diverse the mix, the more potential to expand creativity and build a competitive edge.

## How Diverse is "Diverse"?

Some think "diversity" and envision a mixture of people from different cultures. True diversity indicates virtually every difference imaginable. A few differences include:

| | | |
|---|---|---|
| Age | Gender | Education Level |
| Personal Background | Religion | Work Experience |
| Communication Style | Physical Challenges | Marital Status |
| Lifestyle | Sexual Preference | Personality Type |

Each of these factors — along with dozens of others — impacts how we function in the workplace. Our perspective and experience definitely impact our work style and our contribution to a team. To assemble a team that has the ability to work well together *and* bring the desired results, you need to focus on attracting differences, rather than similarities.

Have you ever been at a meeting where everyone is essentially the "same"? There is no denying that it leads us to essentially agree with all that is being said and go with the status quo. The I-Speak® assessment tool based upon the work of renowned Swiss psychologist Dr. Carl Jung illustrates the impact of different thinking styles. When there is a mix of styles in a communication setting, every base is covered.

I-Speak® categorizes communication styles into four basic types:

Feeler — places a high value on how situations impact people
Intuitor — values ideas, future thinking, creativity and innovation.
Thinker — values statistics, logic and precise procedures.
Senser — gets the job done — implementation and action are their strengths.

In a situation where the team consists of representatives of each style, the outcome is far superior. Imagine planning a new project without someone who will consider every detail along with the consequences upon setup. When the project planning group is made up of a group of intuitors, critical details may be overlooked. And so on.

When you are evaluating your team, look honestly at what the strengths and weaknesses are. Here are a few tips that will guide you in making talent decisions:

Know your own type and be aware of your personal strengths and weaknesses. A couple of valuable assessment tools are the Myers-Briggs® and the disc® By knowing where you excel and what your areas of development are, you can seek out talent that will complement your own style.

Bring several trusted colleagues into the interview process. When one person handles the initial interviewing process, similar candidates tend to crop up. Enlist a couple of trusted colleagues to participate in the first cut of candidates and you will see a fresh perspective about the available talent.

Brainstorm with your team on the "type" of individual who would best fit. Be careful here that you don't outline a specific personality type who will be next to impossible to locate. Rather, look for traits that are missing from the current team mix. Seek out an experience base, or other differences that are lacking.

Behavioral Questions are the most revealing in terms of projecting how people will act and react in the workplace. Since the best predictor of future behavior is past behavior, you will have a much better chance of seeing the *real* person instead of just the typical rehearsed answers.

Take a communication course, which points out your own abilities. Becoming a better listener and honing your ability to connect with all types of individuals will serve you in every facet of your life.

Enroll in a diversity class at least once, in spite of how much you already think you know. Picking up even one new tip or surfacing one stereotype you embrace will make you more successful in finding commonalties rather than emphasizing differences.

Be daring . . . hop out of your comfort zone and try a few of these tips. The resulting team and communication level may bring ideas and innovation that a team made of similar individuals can never conceive of! And your effectiveness as an organization will be dramatically enhanced!

# Baby Boomers Vs.
# Generation-X At Work

---

*"Parents and kids today dress alike,
listen to the same music, and are friends.
Is this a good thing?"*

*— Marilyn Gardner*

---

The Generation Gap has long been talked about. Today, differences between Baby Boomers and Generation X-ers (Gen-Xers) are evident in nearly every aspect of the workplace, the most pronounced of which is the dot-com world.

Gen-Xers seem to dominate the dot-coms, and as some Boomers see it, have skipped the steps of earning their stripes. Many are achieving instant success — or making a lot of money at an early age. Sure, Boomers are proud when these success stories involve their own "brilliant" children. The challenge comes when the two groups come together as coworkers. Then, sparks can fly — especially when the "kids" at work are in charge!

## Role Reversal

In the past, workers played by the corporation's rules. The employer was in charge and valued its employees' talent for longevity and loyalty. When the reorganization decade began, roles reversed and employees started setting many of their own rules. Once the new rules caught on, workers still depending on blind loyalty from their company as a security guarantee were sorely disappointed. Those playing by the new rules switched jobs frequently . . . even over to competitors. Do these workers feel guilty? No way . . . after all, corporate America changed the rules . . . they didn't!

## Supply vs. Demand

In today's market, the demand for skills far outnumbers the availability of talent. More workers are imported from around the world and senior citizens are a vital part of many teams. Companies that integrate their work force with representatives from all experience levels are discovering key differences in attitude, motivation and work styles. Smart organizations leverage their talent by embracing and nurturing these differences.

## Food for Thought

Past motivators were based primarily upon increased responsibility and compensation. A psychological contract of lifetime employment prevailed. Gen-Xers were raised by parents who felt betrayed because they were laid off. Now, growth experiences and stretch assignments are of great interest.

In the old school, self-expression demonstrating personal values was kept to a minimum. Today, body piercings, tattoos and creatively styled and colored hair are widely accepted in the workplace. Look beyond the superficial and there are dozens of commonalities—no matter which era you examine.

Over-communicate! This saying beckons the most coveted commodity—information. In times of constant restructuring, people want and need to be kept informed on a daily basis. In fact, I recommend kicking off each day with a brief team meeting—a huddle—prioritizing projects and dealing with challenges.

Fun was never part of the "deal" under previous work ethics. Workers basically put the yoke on every morning and did whatever was necessary to get the job done. Today's workers expect an environment that supports play and creativity.

Condone balance between work and life. While workers may still be willing to put in overtime, they are less willing to sacrifice everything for their jobs. They have learned that when work comes first, no one suffers more than they do personally. And no one on his or her deathbed says, "I wish I had worked more".

Relate the individual's contribution to the big picture. When assigning tasks, let each person decide how to do the job. Put safety nets in place, but let *them* figure out how to make it all work. Value is added when they realize their part in the organization's overall success.

Make feedback part of the daily routine. Managers need to ensure that employees have everything needed to get their jobs done. In the past, organizations gave formal feedback once a year, by way of performance reviews. By then, missed opportunities were irretrievable.

Radical ideas and proven management skills make a great combination. Gen-Xers started many companies that have grown to the point where input is needed from seasoned leaders, who can take business to the next level. Eliminating the age hierarchy creates an atmosphere of success for all concerned.

Bottom line, both generations should abandon predetermined expectations and merge together as a single working unit in their chosen environment. Keep in mind that the best of all worlds includes a widely diverse base of skills, experience, education and motivation. And yes—age is the path leading to success!

# Breaking Into The Good
# Old Boy's Club

*"Women do everything that men do,
only women do it backwards
and on high heels."*

*— Ginger Rogers*

Fred Astaire is known as one of the premier ballroom dancers of all times. Ginger Rogers, his partner, is known primarily as just that—his partner. Being accepted as part of the Good Old Boy's Club is an ongoing challenge for many businesswomen. And depending on your generation, some of the obstacles may be based upon your subconscious programming of where your "place" is in the world of work.

## A Patriarchal Society

In my generation of Baby Boomers, even though women were entering the workforce in droves, the "Father Knows Best" image prevailed. Women were basically channeled into several fields of work such as teaching, nursing, secretarial and social work.

I can still remember my high school guidance counselor telling me (in spite of my Honor Roll status), that I really didn't need to go to college. After all, HE said I would no doubt be getting married and wouldn't be needing four additional years of school. Luckily, I had more evolved parents who encouraged me to earn a degree.

## Times Change More Quickly than Evolving Attitudes

In government, business, medicine, military, religious organizations and virtually every segment of work, men have been in charge. For those in the Gen-X or the Gen-Y generations, a different message was sent. Females grew up seeing their moms in the workplace and suddenly, virtually every occupation opened up for women and they had unlimited choices.

Trouble is, while doors opened, the men remained in charge. While this is slowly changing, there is still a powerful group of men who rule — the Good Ole Boy's Club. Evolving attitudes do not necessarily mean practice of those attitudes begins immediately. Therefore, the more flexible women are — and the more willing they are to play by the established rules — the more likely it is that the Old Guard will accept them.

While some of the younger businesswomen I work with view this practice as outrageously distasteful, my stance is that sometimes you have to pick your battles and accept reality.

## Proven Strategies

When I first joined the business world, I tried out numerous strategies for being accepted into the Good Ole Boy's Club. I lived in the South where women in business were even scarcer. A few strategies that brought me positive results and enhanced my career are detailed below.

**Understand Men's Motivations.** Women are often motivated by their nurturing instincts. They may concentrate on performing in the work world in order to be liked. The "need to please" can motivate some women to turn back flips for others with no personal gain. Men, on the other hand, are typically more overtly competitive. They constantly look at their place in the pack and vie for power. When women realize that staying until 1 AM to finish up that PowerPointä presentation for a male co-worker's big speech the next day won't result in "extra points", trying to please will become a behavior of the past.

**Tune into Men's Topics.** If you have taken a look at any magazines lately that are geared to male audiences, you no doubt have noticed topics centering around subjects such as power, competition, cars and sports. Women's magazines, on the other hand, tend to center around how to be attractive, accepted, noticed and dress fashionably. Read a few men's periodicals and you can pick up some valuable information, which you can pull out in male dominated discussions. Take up golf, tennis, skeet shooting or a coed sport such as softball, bowling or volleyball and you will build relationships with men in social environments.

**Join Their Clubs.** Becoming an active member of a local Rotary or Lion's Club is an excellent means of meeting men in the business environment. And once you join, you'll need to be active and make significant contributions. Just showing up for the regular meetings isn't going to impress anyone. Working alongside male colleagues on projects will give them an opportunity to see how you operate in terms of creativity, follow-up, attitude and integrity. Building your network with men outside of your own company will ultimately lead to a terrific reputation.

**Network.** Once you have built some contacts in and around your industry, start being aware of how you can support them in succeeding. When you take the initiative to start the exchange of information, it will, in time, begin to flow back downhill to you. Send a male contact a copy of a new and interesting business article with a short note attached. Give them a call and ask them if they are aware of an upcoming meeting that could provide valuable connections. Pass on a lead or contact . . . all without expecting anything in return or keeping score.

**Know YOUR Stuff.** Many women in business have experienced the feeling that they have to work extra hard to prove themselves. That they have to excel just to be taken seriously. My opinion is that this is true . . . but that there is absolutely nothing wrong with striving for excellence. After all, who wins? When you develop your own skills and knowledge to the highest point, you will move up even more quickly.

**Look Like a Woman, but Think Like a Man.** Sometimes, businesswomen are unclear about how to present themselves professionally. A winning strategy is to make the most of your feminine attributes without being overtly sexual. You can present a polished, feminine image without being distracting. And, while in work situations, stick to business. I have attended dozens of meetings and observed women simply wasting time, acting girly, and showing emotions inappropriately. Save this type of behavior for social settings if you are inclined to use them at all.

Following these simple steps will set you on track to be noticed and accepted as a serious individual who means business. a woman who can be counted on to get things done — because you are a *Professional* — not because you are a *Woman*!

# CHAPTER SEVEN

---

# *Skills that Spell*
# *"S-E-C-U-R-I-T-Y"*

# Customer Service With An Attitude

---

*"A pencil is a pencil. It's the service*
*that makes the difference."*

— *Motto for Hillcrest Stationers, San Diego, CA*

---

Typically, the average organization hears from only 4% of their dissatisfied customers. What happens to the other 96%? They simply go away and never come back! Service is the key differentiator between you and your competition.

Building and growing positive relationships is actually much easier than finding new customers. Great customer service relationships result in return visits, repeat orders, good will, loyalty and/or the willingness to recommend your services to others.

When you provide exceptional service to both internal and external customers, a more effective work environment results. And that dynamic further ensures that each customer feels satisfied after every encounter with a team member.

When you begin with a strategy meant to *exceed* customer service expectations, it will impact *all* of an organization's goals. While we hear the buzzwords about service, very few firms truly master the concept of "Customer Obsession".

# Service Jobs on the Rise

Business forecasters have stated that as many as 88% of the labor force currently provides service in some way. That is why it's critical to continue developing *your* skills in this area—you will always be in demand!

# Know Your Customer

In planning how to best serve your clients, take time to research and document your findings. Your research will lead to a clear, in-depth understanding of your customers.

- Are there multiple demographics?
- Are any clients more important than others?
- Is a specific market segment serviced?
- What needs, expectations and recommendations are you hearing that can make your business better?

Remember, customers are not dependent upon your organization. Your firm works for the customers. They deserve your most courteous, attentive and professional treatment. They are the lifeblood of your business. Always remember that without customers, there would be no business!

A happy customer will tell three to five people about their positive experience, but a dissatisfied customer will tell up to 10 people about their negative experience. This means we have to satisfy many more who will pass the word on about our great products or services as a negative testimonial will travel much wider.

# Key Customer Considerations

While every business differs in its particular way of providing good customer service, there are common threads.

The three keys are: *attitude, personal perceptions* and the *acceptance of each customer as an individual.* True, most employees are aware of these points. However, they sometimes simply forget to focus on them daily when relating to customers.

**Attitude** is projected in every interaction we have with others. It can be detected the minute someone looks at you, or as soon as you open your mouth on the phone. It is reflected in voice tone, posture, facial expression, gestures and dozens of other forms of nonverbal communication. We reflect our attitude in all that we do and it cannot be camouflaged. Ask yourself: "Would I want to talk to me?"

The great news about attitude is that you are 100% in control of yours. Whenever you interact with others, you make a choice. You can reflect a positive, upbeat attitude, or you can let other situations that have taken place prior to the interaction impact the current customer. Show a sense of empathy and remember to hear the customer out — no matter what. Thinking back to times when you have experienced bad customer service and how you felt about the person and company that delivered it will help you to avoid acting the same way.

**Perception** can be tricky, because our perception *is* our reality. It is important to be sensitive to differences. Remember, it is not important what you *say*, but what the customer hears and sees. It is not important what you *mean*, but what the customer understands.

Perceptions are not always based on facts and may come from our own prejudices and misperceptions. We may tend to stereotypically think about a person because of a group to which they belong. Or, we may apply the "halo effect." when we generalize that someone must be terrific based on only one experience with them, or their connection with someone we know. If we draw conclusions based on culture, personality or emotions, we are only seeing a fraction of the picture. Take a step back and look at the *big picture*!

**Acceptance of the customer as an individual** is the most important step in providing fantastic service. There is no "right way" to talk to a customer. Each one is different, so look at them as an individual and form a relationship. You should really care about them as a person. Don't just care about *helping* them. Customize the way you communicate to reflect the way the customer will understand. Always listen and pay attention to what you hear from the other party.

By really paying attention and honing this skill, the customer will always tell you exactly what they need. Often, they don't know it themselves, but you can translate, providing improvements and heading off problems. The more you know about them, the better your track record of interpreting their statements. And you'll create new opportunities on every level.

## Using the Information

When applying the three keys — *attitude, perception and acceptance of each customer as unique* — you will receive valuable information. Apply what you have learned to support your relationship with each customer.

- What additional services do they need?
- What mistakes have occurred that may apply to other customers or situations?

It will give you endless chances to learn and gain additional business overall. Your customers always tell you how to get better. Are you listening?

# Telephone Success Skills

*"Telephone etiquette can be summarized
in one word: COURTESY."*

*— Unknown*

U sing the phone is second nature to us. In fact, it's common to see people using the phone while jogging, going through the car wash and in airplanes. "Reach out and touch someone" is a phrase that sounds so simple, yet many of us don't know basic telephone etiquette.

## Using Your Voice

We lose almost all communication cues when talking on the phone; you know—facial expression, body language, eye contact. So it is important to:

- **Begin by putting a big *smile* on your face.** You can hear a smile—it will completely change the tone of your voice and help you to sound enthusiastic and happy to be talking to the person on the other end.
- **Hold the phone about one inch away from your lips**. This will enhance the sound quality and make you sound more like yourself. To really make the most of your voice tone, *stand up*. Think of a business meeting

setting—who has the power? The one standing commands the attention of others. You will feel subconsciously more empowered.

- **Keep your voice calm and relaxed.** When you speak too quickly, you sound stressed and impatient. If possible, lower your volume a little before speaking into the phone, and don't forget to smile before your first words come out!
- **Make a conscious effort to speak clearly and over-enunciate.**
- **Be courteous and give the speaker your undivided attention,**

## Making a Call

- **Immediately identify yourself.** Think about how irritating it is when someone drones on and on while you try to figure out who is calling.
- **Ask Permission.** Always check to see if it is a good time to talk. There is nothing worse than answering the phone and having someone launch into a detailed message while you have someone sitting in your office or are on your way out the door. If they are busy, simply set a time to call back.

## Receiving a Call

- **Try to answer the call** by the second or third ring.
- **Identify yourself** right away.
- **Be a great listener**, showing genuine interest in what the other party is saying.
- **Use their name** in the conversation so they feel a sense of your effort to personalize the discussion.
- If you receive a call-waiting message, **ask permission** from the person you are talking with to put them on hold. Check the incoming call and quickly tell them

when you can call back. Be aware of the person you left in a holding pattern. The time period always seems longer to them than to you.

## Voice Mail

Voice mail is one of the greatest available tools on both a business and personal level, but it is my experience that it is also one of the most misused tools. Leaving messages is one of the best ways to keep communication up to par when we are all dealing with busy schedules and multiple message sources.

## Recorded Incoming Message

- **Keep it short and simple when scripting your voice message.** State your name or at least your number ("Hi, you have reached voice mail for Mark Miller.") This way, the caller has confirmation that they dialed correctly.
- **Remember to give an option** as to where the caller can reach someone "live", in case they have a time-sensitive message.

## Leaving a Meaningful Message

The majority of voice mails I receive tell me *none* of the information I really need, such as:

- Why the person is calling
- What their number is
- When is a good time to call them back

I often check voice mail from my mobile number and don't have my Rolodex handy. It helps me to get back to the caller more quickly when they leave their number each time they call. When giving your number, say it slowly as if giving it to someone who is writing it down. Otherwise, they may have to replay your message to get the number. Mention your name at both the beginning and end of your message—it will save them having to replay as well.

## Leaving Detailed Information

A business associate is different from your best friend. There is no point in leaving a message such as: "Hi, this is Shelly. Give me a call when you can." If the recipient has some indication of the reason for your call, they have the option of responding with what you need.

For example, you could say, "Hi, this is Shelly. I am calling about the 8:30 meeting on Friday. I would like to have five minutes on the agenda to give a project update. Give me a call at 234-4456 and let me know if time allows."

This way, the person can answer your call at any time—even after hours—and cut callbacks to a minimum.

## Closing The Call

Think of the phone as a tool. Get the job done in the least number of calls possible.

When speaking "live", always let the other person hang up first when you say goodbye. You'll never miss a last-minute thought, and it shows great manners.

# E-Mail Etiquette

---

*"Save a tree, send e-mail."*

*– Unknown*

---

If your business experience takes you back ten years or more, you are probably used to a formal tone of business communication. But the with the advent of the most dominant form of information exchange today – e-mail – an entirely new etiquette has emerged.

## Flexibility

E-mail is so "flexible" that it allows us to send a one-sentence response or comment, or attach an entire document. Because it is so immediate (witness instant messaging and chat), exchanges have taken on a more conversational format. Formal grammar rules and sentence structure are bent. Therefore, lots of Internet users get lazy and cut corners to save time.

## Your Image

Remember, when you write and send an e-mail communication in a business setting, you are conveying a message that gives others an opinion of you. Are you detailed and yet concise? Do you follow up quickly? Here are a few guidelines to set you apart from the rookies and make you *shine*!

## Tips and Tricks to Set You Apart From the Crowd

- **Remember, your e-mail communication is forwardable.** Some of the e-mail messages I receive absolutely amaze me. If I forwarded them on to other parties, they could be quite damaging. And we have all seen this happen! Remember, you do not want to put anything in writing that you wouldn't want the world, or your boss, to see.

- **Use descriptive language.** Written communication lacks nonverbal cues, such as varying voice tone and eye contact, that are discernable in face-to-face or telephone encounters. Where possible, use exclamation points, emoticons and examples to express your emotion.

- **Run spell check.** While some flexibility is acceptable when writing e-mail communications, you will benefit from quickly editing every document before clicking the "send" button. By setting your "preferences" to include automatic spell checking, you won't even have to remember to do it!

- **Use sound bites.** Keep in mind that most business people get dozens of e-mails a day. Imagine that you are leaving a brief voice mail; type that in and you will hit the mark.

- **Provide an informative subject.** Give your e-mails an informative title. It will help the recipient determine the content and priority of your message.

- **Enter an appropriate greeting.** Use an appropriate formal greeting to set the best tone. If you don't know the person, address them by "Ms." or "Mr.". If they reply using a first name, you can follow up on a first-name basis.

- **Avoid using UPPERCASE.** Using all caps gives the reader the IMPRESSION THAT YOU ARE SCREAMING!!! Not only is this rude, it is much harder to read text when letters are the same size. When you use regular uppercase and lowercase, the recipient is more apt to accurately interpret your message.

- **Don't forward junk.** Along with the Internet and e-mail came inappropriate jokes, online virus warnings, chain letters and offerings of deals too good to be true, collectively called "spam". Most businesses discourage or prohibit personal use of the company Internet. We all know that employers are legally permitted to access our messages and files at will. Try limiting fun messages to peoples' home addresses.

- **Remove unneeded information from your message.** Remember, the idea is to make communication faster and easier. When you forward needless information, you are overloading the Internet with useless noise. Whether replying to or forwarding a message, remove all unnecessary text. No one wants to scroll down 10 pages to get to a two-line message. Use the cut-and-paste feature and the recipients of your messages will appreciate it.

- **Reply in a timely fashion.** If you need an *immediate* answer to a communication, pick up the phone, rather than use e-mail. E-mail puts you in the position of *waiting* for a response. Generally, you should respond to e-mail messages within five days. Since you do not usually know when the person retrieves your message, give them a few days to respond. If you need a quick answer, send it with a high priority flag.

- **Sign off courteously.** Leave your reader with a "thank you", a closing word or a phrase along with your name. On business correspondence, include your title and company name underneath. On the next line, I recommend listing your phone and fax numbers and e-mail address. This will make it much easier for the reader to follow up with you. **Tip**: Don't include such items as a company logo or a graphical "business card" in your signature. Many times the recipient's e-mail will not display it and it adds file size "weight" to the message.

Using these simple tips will make your e-mail correspondence professional and accurate, and will ensure that the world receives the best possible impression of you and your skills!

# Meetings That Work!

*"Meetings are the windows to an organization's culture."*

*— W.R. Daniels & J.G.Mathers*

Meetings can be one of the most dreaded activities scheduled in our Daytimers. You know the type of meetings to which I am referring — the ones that last longer than scheduled, even though nothing is being accomplished. You have to pinch yourself to avoid falling asleep.

## Meeting Facts

Meetings are such notorious time-wasters that groups have even conducted studies on the subject. The Wharton Center for Applied Research recently published their findings in the *Wall Street Journal*:

| Position | Average Hours Per Week in Meetings |
|---|---|
| Chief Executive Officer | 17 hours |
| Senior Executive | 23 hours |
| Middle Manager | 11 hours |

The startling revelation was that only **slightly more than half of the meetings were productive**. In addition, they learned that a memo or voice mail could have replaced over 25% of the meetings!

When we do the math, it is obvious that if meeting time were better spent, there would be more time to get real work done. The study estimated that an organization could save up to $16K annually *per manager* by planning meetings more effectively!

## Meeting Facilitation Secrets

With time at a premium, the more advance planning you put into a meeting, the better the results. Here are several tips to ensure that your meetings work:

- **Begin by carefully considering who really needs to be there.** Fewer participants will result in more progress. When larger groups meet (more than eight participants), productivity starts dropping.
- **Set a specific time frame and stick to it.** If business has been covered with time remaining, go ahead and end the meeting. People will be delighted if the meeting ends early, resulting in "found" time to accomplish something else.
- **Decide desired outcomes in advance.** Set priorities for agenda items. Keep discussions both on track and results-oriented.
- **Distribute a draft of the meeting agenda a day or two in advance.** Invite participants to submit additional items for discussion prior to the meeting time. Set up a flip chart in the meeting room for participants to add to the agenda as they arrive.
- **Pick the right location.** Ensure that the meeting location provides adequate space, a white board or flip chart for recording notes, and can be closed off to provide confidentiality. Bring along a few toys, such as Play-Doh, Slinkys, pick-up sticks or squoosh balls.

Toys break the ice, set the tone for openness and creativity, and allow for some fun.

- **Dedicate the first five minutes of the meeting to sharing good news**, positive results and a quick laugh or two. Invite team members to make announcements about notable activities and goals met since the group was last together.

- **Enlist one participant to act as recorder and write summary notes.** The primary purpose is to keep a record of discussion and actions. Another is to provide those unable to attend the meeting with details of actions and follow-up items. Distribute the notes to all participants — not just those unable to attend. They serve as a terrific reminder about follow-up. Set up a notebook containing all notes as a historical record, so no matter when a person joins the team, they will be able to use the document to come up to speed.

- **Set an atmosphere of openness.** Ask questions and practice active listening. When decisions are made, summarize the key points to ensure everyone's understanding. You are the facilitator — not an active participant in the meeting. In this role, keep your opinions to yourself and allow the group to express themselves freely.

- **Create action items for follow-up.** Set time frames for completion of all items and delegate the person handling the task. Include brainstorming time for each topic. If time is short, limit this to five minutes, capture ideas and appoint someone to follow up.

- **Begin composing the agenda for the next meeting.** List all items to be carried over and agree on goals for implementation.

- **Close by setting the date and time for the next meeting** so that everyone can make note of it. This will ensure their availability *before* the fact!

If you invest time in planning and preparation *prior* to meetings, you will soon become known for holding meetings that are productive, fun and a terrific use of time.

# Problem Solving Strategies

---

*"Problems are only opportunities
in work clothes."*

— Henry J. Kaiser

---

More often than not, there are many ways to address any problem. Remember, obstacles are 10% what happens in our lives and 90% how we react to what happens. We have all been faced with situations that felt overwhelming. The trick is to use these situations as learning opportunities and build on them as we are faced with new challenges in the future.

## You Can Run, But You Can't Hide!

Truth is, we often run from our problems, hide from them, mask them, self-medicate or hope they will just miraculously take care of themselves. If you have ever found yourself reacting this way, let me make one point perfectly clear. If you don't recognize and take action on problems as they occur . . . and head new ones off at the pass, you will end up spending the majority of your time reacting and putting out fires.

# What Do We Worry About?

While a problem can be simple or complicated to solve, most problems boil down to four basic areas. These areas are related in some way to money, health, loss of some sort, or physical appearance. Would you believe that the number one thing that people worry about is their natural born looks?

In order to turn around problems, we sometimes have to go to the absolute lowest point. Let's face it, at that juncture, we have nothing left to lose. We can relax and take action with more belief that the steps we take will solve our problem—it can't get worse. When we put our problems into perspective, we can break through indecision or fear and take action.

## Components of Problem Solving

To solve essentially any problem effectively, I recommend following five basic steps. Even if you have been faced with a similar problem in the past, it's always a good idea to take time to follow through the steps and consider both the worst and best case outcomes.

- **Analyze and Define the Problem.** How did the dilemma occur or crop up? What exactly is the entire scope of the problem? Write it down—it will be easier to grasp when you can see it on paper. Avoid placing blame for the problem—on others—or even on yourself. Blame simply doesn't accomplish anything. If you are blaming someone else, resentments will crop up. If you blame yourself, your confidence will diminish. Get to the real core of the problem . . . where and how did it start? What are all facets of the situation?

- **Generate Alternatives.** Don't hold back. Brainstorm freely and write out options that cover every base. Consider solutions that are logical, unreasonable, ridiculous, substantial, pie in the sky and realistic. When you allow your mind to just flow, you'll sometimes hit on a potential solution you had not previously considered — and it may actually work. Consider the worst-case scenario and the ideal solution.

   Call in an expert if you need to. Discuss the situation with a colleague or friend who has knowledge of the subject. Think through the domino effect. Will your decision create a chain reaction that will cause even more damage in the long run?
- **Decide on Your Course of Action.** When making your decision about your course of action, depersonalize the decision. How would you advise another person to handle the problem if you had absolutely no stake in the outcome?

   Will the decision take you closer to your overall goals or just sidestep and take you off in another direction? Once you are firm on your solution, if time allows, sleep on your decision. Pay attention to your gut feeling — more often than not . . . it is significant.
- **Follow-though.** OK, this is the challenging step. This is the step where some of us falter. If you start second-guessing at this stage, the entire process will fall apart. You'll be paralyzed with indecision and doubt. There are always multiple ways to solve any problem. Stick with the course of action you have selected and take it all the way to the bank. Do what you say you will do, Period!
- **Evaluate.** After implementing your course of action, wait awhile. Try it on and give your decision time to settle in. Debrief on your problem solving process.

What did you learn? What can you do to ensure the same problem doesn't develop again in the future?

If you decide later that the solution you selected was not the best choice, you can always go back. It is rarely too late to regroup and take a different course of action. Many problems need to be addressed more than once. When you use each course of action as part of your overall learning process, there is never, ever a failure.

Life is made up of one problem after another. Learn how to effectively solve situations as they arise and use them as experiences to build upon for the future. We all choose whether we use our problems as opportunities to grow. Whether we choose to use our street smarts to solve problems or allow them to bury us. Embrace your problems. And let them inspire you to greatness!

# Presentations That Pop!

---

*"How well we communicate is determined not by how well we say things but how well we are understood."*

— *Andrew Grove*

---

There are so many dangers in our daily lives, like going to work each morning on the freeway and watching for unforeseen dangers at speeds of up to 90 mph. Yet, the number one human fear is public speaking! Yes, the typical human would rather be the "guest of honor" at a funeral than the one delivering the eulogy!

You have already discovered that verbally expressing yourself and selling your talents are skills you can never absolutely *perfect*! You may be an exception to the rule, yet you can always consider putting some zing into your presentations with updated materials, jokes, real-life stories and statistics.

## Getting Started—Content

Once you have selected your topic, start writing about it. Go to the computer and do a data dump by putting down every thought you have on the topic—using keywords to remind you of examples, etc. Pull together all your articles, books and notes, and just start writing. Make footnotes for statistics and any material you think you may quote. Ignore grammar for now, as well as content order. Just allow yourself to think of everything you know about the topic. As you make notes, you will be able to extract key threads and headers.

## Who's Listening?

Now, put some thought into who will be tuning in to your brilliant talk. Write down everything you know about them—age, gender, cultural mix, educational level and commonalities. Connecting with your listeners and making your information relevant to them can make or break your speech. Ask any and everyone you know what *they* would want to know about your subject if *they* were in the audience. Don't get too involved with your own idea of what to talk about—a common symptom of a boring speech. Be flexible and open to changing your outline if feedback points you in a different direction.

## What's Your Point?

To get the creative part of your presentation rolling, select the main objective and purpose of your speech, and determine why someone would be inclined to listen to you. Will they:

- Learn how to do something?
- Be persuaded to a new point of view?
- Be motivated to take action?

Write down your objective in clear, concise words, such as: *"The audience will learn the steps necessary to write their own powerful presentation."*

# Start Digging—Research

Of course, the ideal technique is to jump onto your Internet connection, use your favorite search engines to research your topic and add up-to-the-minute statistics. But, you need to be cautious about the sources of information. There is plenty of misinformation available on the Net. And don't forget to keep a record of your sources to back up information. A good way to do this is to print everything and then highlight it. Next, add specifics to your notes as you read.

Some folks head to their local libraries, where there are unlimited periodicals and research sources, as well as expert assistance. Partnering with a resource specialist usually produces fascinating and more detailed information.

# Select Your Key Points

Now that you have identified your objective and purpose, select three to five key points to develop. For example: *"My mission is to present five key strategies that will enable your organization to attract top talent."*

Read over all of your idea files, articles, tables of content from reference books and your highlighted notes. Select themes that are aligned with your mission. For example, if organizational recruitment is the topic, your five critical points may be:

- Building a Corporate Culture
- Leading by Example
- Motivating Your Staff
- Creating a Learning Organization
- Rewarding Your Employees

# Making Content Out of Your Notes

The best way to create your content is to get it down on paper. Review all of your information and let your thoughts flow freely. Add your own life experiences and stories. Before you know it, you will have pages of content supporting your topic.

Jot down thoughts and phrases. An oral presentation needs spontaneity to really flow; so the less rigid you are in your writing, the more "real" you will appear when delivering the content.

Also, if you lose your place when presenting, you can rely on being conversational to pick up speed again.

When you have enough content for your time allowance, try practicing out loud; you will know where to begin splicing and dicing.

## Your Grand Entrance

The opening is definitely the time to grab your listeners. There are many techniques to try:

- Throw out a startling statistic
- Tell a story, serious or humorous
- Use an anecdote to open your topic
- Get the audience physically involved by asking them to stand up and carry out a group action
- Ask a question to get them thinking about your upcoming presentation

## Now, Mix it Up!

Get your audience involved. Invite an audience member to participate in a brief Q&A or share an experience. Or try using props, humor and games. Sharing a story about yourself, especially one that shows vulnerability or humor, gains instant rapport. Get the audience moving by having them interact briefly with one another.

## And Your Grand Finale

Determine how you want to *leave* your audience. First, quickly summarize your points so they are reinforced. Follow with a story or quote, driving your key points home. Or state a call to action, so the listeners leave motivated to do something. If you can come up with a humorous anecdote, leaving them laughing is a great technique to ensure they remember you.

Now you are ready to wow any audience! One final piece of advice: *"A poor speaker quits talking when he is tired. A good speaker quits before the audience is tired!"*

# Writing Great Business Letters

---

*"Words that affect your reader positively are likely to produce the response you desire in letter-writing situations."*

*— Perdue University*

---

Have you been tapped to write the marketing letter for a new account? Are you launching a job search? Or do you need to write follow-up letters to clients? Whatever your objective, you want to shine. And the fact is that what you create in writing can build a professional, efficient impression. Unfortunately, it can also sink you.

Writing is a necessary skill for any professional to consistently practice. In reality, when most of us take that required college writing course, it marks the end of our training. It may be time to brush up, so let's take a quick look at business writing basics.

## Know Your Purpose

Why are you writing? You need to let readers know within the first two lines exactly why they would want to read on. Powerful, direct writing inspires confidence and tells the reader you provide quality in everything you do. The shorter your letter is, the more likely it is to be read.

Stick to a few topics and use brief sentences. Arouse interest, give the facts and remember that less is more. Focus on your readers and what you think they would most likely want to hear.

## Tone—Write Like You Speak

A mistake many of us make is to create documents that are simply too formal—too "correct"—and thus, stilted. Use the same tone in writing that you use when talking. Leave the $50 words at home and stick to language that is descriptive, concise and action-oriented.

Be assertive—avoid using words and phrases such as "it is my understanding," "I feel" or "could". Avoid abstract ideas and use examples to illustrate actions or plans. When you make your sentences come alive with examples, people will be much more likely to remember what you wrote.

## Use Correct Names and Titles

When writing a letter to a male, we don't designate whether he is married or single, so follow the same rule with women. Address all women as "Ms." When you're unsure of the person's title or the spelling of a name, give the company a call and *ask*. It is offensive to the person receiving a piece of correspondence if their name is misspelled.

A businesswoman friend whom I greatly admire held numerous high-level banking positions. It was during the time when those roles were strongly dominated by males. She has a very unusual name, and if she received a piece of correspondence addressed to "Mr.", she wouldn't respond to it—especially if it was a networking or job inquiry. She felt that if the writer didn't even take time to find out whether she was male or female, or to spell her name correctly, she didn't have time to meet with them. I have to admit, I agree!

## Accentuate the Positive

Appeal to the positive side by using affirmative, rather than negative, language. Readers will respond more favorably and feel a sense of goodwill. Emphasize what *is*, rather than what is *not*. Avoid words with negative connotations, such as "not", "loss" and "unfortunately". Use positive language instead. And put the information you want to emphasize at the top or bottom of paragraphs.

## Call to Action

Once you have written your information, you want your audience to *do* something. What is that? Be motivated to change something? Be persuaded? Learn something new? Hire you? This is the part where you call the reader to action. Be assertive. Let them know exactly what you want them to do when they finish reading. If you tell them directly, they are much more likely to do it.

When writing job search related correspondence, I recommend ending your letter with a statement of what you will do to follow up. If you give the recipient the "task" of following up with you, you will end up waiting, not knowing what will happen next.

End your letter by saying that you will give them a call to learn more about their needs and how your skills can support their company in reaching its goals. Then, without fail, follow up. It is the "kiss of death" not to do something you said you were going to do.

## Edit and Edit Again

Except for the most basic documents, I strongly recommend spending time between drafting and finalizing your writing. What works best for me is to first formulate the idea, and then edit and enrich the content by ensuring my information is properly organized. Then I cut out the fluff—anything not absolutely necessary.

After that, I print out the piece and let it settle for an hour or so. Then I go back and read it later, making handwritten edits and notes in the margin. Lastly, I make any changes and read it one more time before I print out my final copy. We tend to pick up fewer errors when we write *and* edit our own work, so if possible, have a colleague read over your final version.

Following these simple rules should help you steer right to the point and get your letters read, resulting in action!

# Skills—Your Secret Weapon

*"We're living in turbulent times because we
are caught up in a world of changing
paradigms. In times of change, learners inherit
the earth while the learned are often simply
beautifully equipped to
lead a world that no longer exists.
Stay in school all your life!"*

*— Eric Hoffer*

$\mathrm{B}$ack in the days of the cave man, the name of the game was "survival of the fittest". In today's work jungle, survival hinges on skills. He/she who has the most cutting-edge skills, ranking highest in comparison to their peers, will inherit the best jobs. In the current work environment, we are constantly marketing our specific competencies, so being stagnant just isn't an option for the successful.

In my career development work, one complaint I hear over and over again from hiring managers and recruiters is that candidates cannot clearly and concisely state their skills. It is even harder for them to get to the second step, which is showing an organization how their skills can be of value to *them*. When asked about our talents and accomplishments, most of us tend to shuffle our feet and say, "Oh, I was just doing my job".

I'll loosely define a "skill" as a learned capability that allows us to get things done in the world. We all have numerous skills, but the key is to learn which ones are in demand, and then outline our accomplishments surrounding them. We usually stop with just listing them . . . and miss the opportunity to market how we connect and use them.

## Types of Skills

Skills are generally classified into four key areas—people, things, ideas and data. Of those broad areas, with which do you feel most motivated? Here are some examples of each area, along with representative work:

| | Skill | Type of Work |
|---|---|---|
| **People** | Consulting, Advising, Selling, Organizing | Buyer, Customer Service Rep, Teacher, Sales Rep |
| **Things** | Tooling, Drafting, Constructing, Inspecting | Engineer, Pilot, Machinist, Installer, X-Ray Tech |
| **Ideas** | Problem-solving, Writing, Inventing, Planning | Architect, Chemist, Programmer, Graphic Artist |
| **Data** | Auditing, Budgeting, Computing, Research | Accountant, Teller, Mail Clerk, Editor, Data Entry Operator |

## Motivated Skills

As our experience base grows, so does our skill base, which means we need to constantly prune back what we are marketing. That is, take time to list and then prioritize your skills. Which are you *motivated* to use on a daily basis and which do you dread because of burnout? The dreaded skills can always be pulled out in a pinch, or mentioned in an interview situation, if it will put you at a competitive advantage.

When you find flow in what you do, when you lose track of time, you are operating at peak capacity. Continue to challenge yourself to keep learning so you will always be motivated adding new skills to your repertoire. Why not choose to work in an environment where you are motivated, always doing what you love?

## Updating Skills

Once you have identified your motivating skills, take the exercise a step further and make note of any skill area you need to update. Also, list any areas in which you need to acquire new skills. If any one side of your work skills is out of balance, will it impact your career in the future? Adding new talents to your skill base will ensure that you are always marketable and in demand. Look for upcoming trends and niches where you can advance and keep planning your next steps.

We all have unlimited opportunities to learn and develop new talents. The days of finishing school and working for the next 30-40 years without learning anything else are long gone.

Remember that your future is best guided by your past. To what do you gravitate and feel most comfortable doing? While our employers support us in learning new skills, we are ultimately responsible to make sure this happens, because we take them with us as we move from job to job.

Continually learn—and become very competent at the things you love to do. Make sure you know the dollar value of your skills in the marketplace. Finally, be open to moving your skills from opportunity to opportunity. With this formula, you will be both successful and well rewarded in your career.

# CHAPTER EIGHT

# Work Place Politics, Relationships and Schmoozing

# Being Politically Correct at the Office

---

*"Even when you're out to get something*
*done — not to do someone in —*
*you have to play politics."*

— Michael Warshaw, *Fast Company*

---

The word "sycophant" hadn't entered my vocabulary —
not through reading, movies, TV or my own experiences.
Then along came Dilbert . . . and while I had known there
*must* be a word for the unabashed yes-man, there it was in
writing! A word for the "Eddie Haskells" of the world —
the person(s) in every office who misses no opportunity to
promote themselves, steal the credit due others or suck up
to the boss.

## I Hate Politics

For the past decade, I have had the privilege of coaching
people from all walks of life and levels of work responsibility.
The one common thread I hear is, "Politics . . . I hate it".
Another shared lament — "The reason my job was
eliminated was politics." Politics are here to stay . . . so get
over it! Learn the rules and play to your comfort level. One
reality we all know is that when *we* are on the right side of
those in power, we think politics are pretty cool!

# The Great Truths of Politicking

The first great truth is that politics mean nothing more than communication. It is all about integrity and honesty — or the lack thereof. We all know the ultimate suck-up who seems to get the best assignments. If you stay on track and apply the following guidelines, you will be noticed and become *painlessly* successful at politics.

## Play Fair

If you send out negative information about others, be prepared to hear unsavory things about yourself. It goes both ways! Remember the adage, "What goes around, comes around." Speculating just for the fun of it can cause others undue pain, so be selective if you make the choice to pass on any gossip.

## Build and Nurture Relationships

You can always be part of a work colleague's professional network, so keep communication lines open and tune in to what is happening to others around you. You might begin to understand their points of view. You don't have to *like* someone to work with them. And you never know when someone you despise could end up being your boss.

## Be a Trusted Confidant

We all need to vent occasionally. If a colleague bends your ear, keep it confidential. You will earn valuable respect. And limit the number of people listening to you moan and whine!

## Assume that Others are Well-intended

Most of us have made remarks that others misinterpreted. If a colleague says something that rubs you the wrong way, let him or her know; then ask to discuss it privately. Usually, the air can be easily cleared. Now, move on and wipe the slate clean. Harboring grudges is a mistake and wastes too much energy!

## Keep Your Personal Life Personal

Work relationships are terrific and can be extended to occasional outings, such as dinner. But avoid getting too friendly with coworkers. Dating and breaking up can create awkward situations. Or you may regret disclosing personal information after a few beers at happy hour. Limit personal soul-searching to family members and close friends.

## Do What You Say You are Going to Do

Following through is the best way to get key players in any organization to notice you. Present information on time, make it better than required and keep your word. If you remark, "I'll give you a call", then *call* the person!

## Inform Management of Your Progress

It is never too late to start advising your manager of present and past accomplishments. Sitting quietly and expecting your manager to "notice what you do" just because "that's the boss's job" will ensure that you wait a long time for recognition! The more you let your manager know about you, the more comfortable he/she will be with your skills and potential!

## Keep Developing Your Communication Skills

Communication skills — writing, listening *and* talking — require constant practice. The more you understand others' personality types, the more you will be able to adapt and appeal to their particular style.

## Ask for Input and Advice from Your Managers

Asking for feedback will teach you a great deal. If you are just looking for strokes or an opportunity to define your position, don't even bother asking. Be prepared to hear input you don't necessarily want to hear. Use the information to better your image and polish any rough areas.

## Document Facts and Events

Bill Gates advises to conduct negotiations and decision-making via e-mail. He says that it provides faster follow-up and accountability. It really does work great—and there is never a question of who said what or who is supposed to do what.

## Be a Bright Spot in the Environment

*Choosing* to be positive and pleasant is up to each person. No matter what's going on in your life, keeping an even temperament at work is a minimum requirement. Why not take it a step further and be memorable as someone always terrific to be around?

## Beware of Finding Fault with Other People— Especially in Front of Others

It is fine to see better ways of doing things, but remember that the grapevine distorts information and you may end up on the hot seat. The saying, "Never say anything out loud that you wouldn't want to see printed on the front page of the newspaper", sums it all up!

None of us can practice all of the golden truths of office politics at all times. There will always be an inevitable slip-up or oversight. If you make it your best practice to earn the respect of others by being up-front and honest, it will bolster your visibility on *every* level!

# The Company Party

---

*"In do-your-own-thing America, there is no longer much distinction between etiquette, the rules of behavior, and manners, the social premises from which they are derived."*

— *Miss Manners*

---

Time for the annual company party or convention? View the party as a work event—you will be observed and remembered for your conduct. If you end up dancing with the lampshade on your head, it will be hard to live down.

Here are a few tips to make business-related social events work *for* your career.

## DOs

- **DO go alone** unless you have a spouse or a significant other. If you make the mistake of just taking a date for the sake of a date, you will spend lots of time introducing and trying to make sure your date is having a good time instead of focusing on the opportunity to network.
- **DO view this as an opportunity** to get to know others within the company. Mingle and mix and ask

lots of open-ended questions about topics like work, friends, sports, other companies, and world events.

- **DO make an effort to introduce yourself** to the spouses/guests of your colleagues. It can be difficult to be the "stranger" at an event—people will remember your friendliness.
- **DO arrive within 30 minutes of the start of the event**, unless there is a pre-event cocktail hour. Often, presentations, welcoming addresses and/or introductions are made, and showing up "whenever" is rude.
- **DO lighten up on the alcohol.** Just because it's an open bar doesn't mean you should take the opportunity to drink as much free liquor you can. There's nothing worse than having someone ask you about something that happened at the party and having no recollection of what they're talking about. It makes you wonder what else you might have said or done that you don't remember. Keep it low key, and you will be able to remember everything that happens!
- **DO follow up with thanks after the party.** A great way to leave people with a positive impression is to write a note to the organizers of—or the person responsible for—the party afterward. Let them know how much you appreciated their work and planning. If you work for a small company, go direct to the top with your thanks.

## DON'Ts

- **DON'T take a plastic bag to fill up with food** from the buffet!
- **DON'T dress like you are going out to attract your ideal mate.** While special events offer the opportunity to "dress up", you want to be remembered for what

you talk about and what you ask rather than your unbelievably revealing outfit. The goal here is to celebrate with your coworkers, not to be a sex symbol. **Rule of thumb:** if you have to doubts about your choice of attire, skip it and choose something else.

- **DON'T use this forum as an opportunity to try out your stand-up comic routine** with all of your hot new off-color jokes.
- **DON'T ask personal questions** or bring up sensitive topics like religion, politics, salary, "how big was YOUR Christmas bonus", etc.
- **DON'T spend the evening hanging with your friends** and ignoring others. You see your friends every day . . . and may not have an opportunity to mingle with some of the other folks on a daily basis.
- **DON'T pick this event as the time to go home with a co-worker** for the first time just because you are feeling jolly. You may regret it later. If it is meant to be, it will "keep" a few days!
- **DON'T seize this as your opportunity to show off your new "dirty dancing" routine.** Being conservative will make a much more positive impression!
- **DON'T eat and run.** Just as arriving late is frowned upon, leaving too early can also give the wrong impression. Don't eat and cut out immediately to "relieve the babysitter" or to attend another event. Wait until the post-meal activities begin and surreptitiously make your exit.
- **DON'T make off with the centerpieces**, etc. just because "somebody has to take them home". Au contraire . . . leave with a big thank you to your hosts and that's it.

Follow these tips and you will have no company party-related regrets — just opportunities to make a great impression.

# Love And Labor—A Toxic Mix?

*"Friendship often ends in love; but love in friendship — never."*

*— Charles Colton*

The debate about workplace romance has raged for years . . . should companies tolerate it . . . or look the other way? If your organization *doesn't* have a written policy on the subject, it is part of the norm. According to a 1998 SHRM (Society of Human Resource Management) survey, 87% of firms polled don't. It is a theme, however, that companies should address in one way or another to avoid litigation.

Today's professional expects more balance between work and personal life. My observation is that there are even some who want "one stop shopping" by blending personal and professional aspects. Many put so much energy into commuting and working that they have little time left over to meet someone and date. This makes the work realm the obvious hunting ground.

The key challenge in regulating this issue is that, simply put, the individuals involved determine whether or not problems will occur before, during or after an office fling. When a company makes subjective judgments about employee behavior, trouble begins to brew.

Let's consider first *why* romances spring up between cubicle walls. The setting is groups of people with like interests working side-by-side in a creative and challenging intellectual environment. It is pure nature that the most basic human attraction kicks in at some point. Trouble arises when it happens between people who are already married, or perhaps a manager and subordinate. It seems to me that when office romance is good . . . it is very, very *good*. But when it goes bad . . . which, let's face it, it usually does . . . it is very, very *bad*!

## Why Can't Firms Regulate Romance?

Some people involved in workplace romances handle themselves just fine; others make a mess of it. In the meantime, if the employee performs his/her duties in a productive manner, the company doesn't have a leg to stand on without a formal written policy. You *can*, however, oppose any relationships that impact organizational goals.

## Morale

A romance between two team members will undoubtedly be obvious to others at some point. No matter how secretive they are, word will get out and can affect the morale of coworkers. Others may sense a loss of openness in team communication, which leads inevitably to gossip and speculation. If the two lovebirds are open about their relationship, others often end up knowing more details than they care to. Overall, the group dynamic is dramatically altered . . . especially if one player is the manager!

## Favoritism

When a manager is involved with a subordinate, there is even more room for trouble to brew. Coworkers will undoubtedly think the apple of the manager's eye is receiving special treatment. Bottom line, in the long run, the employee can be overlooked for promotions or special assignments—even when they are the most qualified—if the manager overcompensates by wanting to appear fair to everyone else.

## Productivity

Ultimately, love at work can impact productivity. Charles Pierce, professor of psychology at Montana State, maintains that scientific data shows workplace romances can sometimes result in productive employees. We all know that rush of falling in love . . . but we also know that it is impossible to maintain over the long term. When things are going well, productivity may actually increase, but if it turns sour, productivity will be affected across the board in a negative way.

## The Harassment Card

This is the wild card—when love interests develop, harassment charges can pop up from all angles. Coworkers can file suit if a sexually charged work environment makes them uncomfortable. Even being subjected to coworkers' innuendoes can result in a harassment charge. If the love interest wanes, a subordinate can accuse the manager of using the inside information against them when it comes time for a promotion. The scenarios are endless.

## So What's A Company To Do?

Establish a clear, fair, unwritten policy. Make it lenient to avoid having to make subjective judgments about employee behavior. When employees step over the bounds of better judgment, nip the problem in the bud. Constantly remind them why they are at work. They are there to be taken seriously—to make a contribution. Viewing coworkers as sex objects is not conducive to working side-by-side. Expecting your employees to maintain a professional demeanor and atmosphere isn't asking too much . . . it is a minimum requirement. Remember that the corporate world is **not** democratic.

When situations arise, evaluate them on a case-by-case basis. In most instances, if an organization has a problem with one employee involved romantically with a coworker, they end up having problems with two employees! Remember, employees are on board to support the company in reaching goals—not to live out their personal fantasies!

Overall, the best measure is to discourage workplace romances. The words of E. M. Forster say it best—"Love is a great force in private life; it is indeed the greatest of all things; but love in public affairs does not work".

# Establishing Credibility
# With Male Colleagues

---

*"If one is careless about basic things—telling
the truth, respecting moral codes, proper
professional conduct—who can believe them
on other issues?"*

*— James L. Hayes*

---

As long as women are considered to be a minority in the business world, they will continue to face the challenge of establishing credibility with some of their male colleagues. This situation has changed dramatically over the past two decades, proving this obstacle will lessen over time.

## Changing Roles in the World of Work

The credibility challenge was created in a large part due to the dramatic role changes of women and men over the past 50+ years. While the world is still dominated by males in virtually all areas of power, women are making more contributions and breaking new ground at an amazing pace. The "Catch 22" is that many of the men in the power roles are from the old school and still see women as unable to hold leadership roles. The good news is that the younger generations represented in today's workforce have a strong tendency to accept an individual for their skills—not for their gender.

I am a Baby Boomer who spent much of my career in the southeast in male dominated work environments. During this time, I have observed and experienced many unique situations where women's work abilities were pre-judged as lightweight or substandard by men simply because they were women. The good news is that there are many ways to overcome this challenge. Here are a few strategies that have worked for many successful businesswomen.

## Understand Your Male Colleagues

The best strategy for working around the biases of others is to understand the person's perspective. Take a look at the men who can most support you and those who can potentially be obstacles to your progress. Examine where they are coming from and make a strong attempt to "walk a mile in their shoes".

For example, if the male is in his late 50's or older, he may well have grown up with his mom waiting at home to serve milk and cookies when he arrived home from school. He may well have read the work of Martin Luther stating, "Women are a stupid vessel over whom men must always hold power". And, his programming, in spite of the obvious changes in the world, will typically default him to that stance. Keeping it in mind that his actions and comments are *not personal* will allow you to maintain your professional demeanor. Remember, some day *we* may be the one with the old-fashioned ideas!

## Become a True Expert in Your Field

Practicing continuous learning and striving to be an absolute authority in your field of expertise is a win-win strategy.

You will advance and be more accepted by men who may have held the positions of expert in the past. I was recently talking with a 40-something male scientist who was interviewing for a position where he would be working under the direction of a female. It was refreshing to hear him remark more than once "she is the smartest scientist I have ever known—working for her would be such a learning experience." He didn't say she was the smartest *woman* scientist. It struck me that in spite of his generation, he had evolved beyond considering gender when evaluating ability.

## Exude Confidence

One trait that many women wear openly is modesty—not bragging about ourselves, not drawing attention to our accomplishments. This is a losing strategy. While arrogance is unattractive in any gender, owning your accomplishments and stepping into your power is always attractive to others— regardless of gender. An excellent book titled *The Confident Woman* by Marjorie Hansen Shaevitz drives home the fact that confidence can be built by our actions and thoughts. Making mistakes and learning from them is part of the scenario, so remember to revel in and learn from every experience.

## Develop Terrific Communication Skills

We all have different styles of communicating with others. The style we develop is influenced by many things including where we were raised, our educational background, our personal experiences, our age, and yes, even our gender. Keep the premise of "male logic" and "female intuition" in mind when communicating. Stick to the facts and back them up with examples. Avoid using words such as "I feel" and go for the straightforward statement. Being direct will definitely make a difference in your communication outcomes.

Using polite speech in business communications can be interpreted as a lack of assertiveness. Men tend to simply state their opinion while women often use "tag" phrases such as "if you are OK with that". And don't tolerate interruptions when you are speaking just to be polite. Use assertive mannerisms such as good eye contact and unclasped hands. Oh, and leave the nervous giggle at home.

## Dress the Part

If you want to be perceived and accepted as a player, you absolutely have to look the part. Think of all the situations where others will observe you, but won't actually speak to you. Or see you make a presentation, but not meet you one-on-one. First impressions are made in a split second, and they are lasting.

Today's ever-causal business environment invites women to dress down and in my opinion, this can mean giving up some power. Cute dresses, strappy sandals, sleeveless tops and cleavage just don't cut it in the work environment. Sure, you will definitely be *noticed*, but you may not be taken seriously and respected.

Women often are their own worst obstacle in this area — we are programmed to think we need to look pretty, attract the attention of males and show our feminine side. I recommend showing your feminine side . . . but keeping it a bit more formal. Try wearing a jacket over your casual slacks or wearing more powerful colors such as red or royal blue rather than yellow or pink. Save the open toed shoes and spike heels for social events and keep your jewelry to a minimum. Remember, the adage "less is more" works like a charm when make-up, big hair and perfumes are concerned.

The "product" you are offering to the world must be who you *truly* are . . . all the time. If you simply *create* a role to please others, you can never be fully comfortable in that role. Strive to improve yourself in every way, and be proud of your expertise. Your "star quality" will shine through and make you memorable to your colleagues — regardless of gender!

# Working For A Woman Boss

---

*"Leadership is not gender-oriented—it is a combination of skills and traits that allow an individual to bring others together for a common purpose."*

— *Camille Primm*

---

Today's dynamic workplace offers leadership roles to those who can consistently show *results*. The days of appointing someone just because they are the senior person, the obligatory female or the owner's nephew are gone.

When discussing their work situations, I often hear men say that reporting to a woman boss . . . especially one younger . . . can be challenging. Hmmm. Let's face it; we *all* have our rough areas. The trick is to understand the individual, their motivations and how best to communicate with them.

## The Woman's Perspective

Throughout history, women have been hard workers who place high value on achievement. They often value their personal worth based upon their accomplishments, rather than how much money they make or whether they wield power.

*I don't know anything about luck. I've never
banked on it, and I'm afraid of people who do.
Luck to me is something else: hard work and
realizing what is opportunity and what isn't."*

—Lucille Ball

"Acting out", being girlie or temperamental simply
won't work with most women bosses. Stepping up to the
plate and accepting accountability will.

## The Big Boys' Opinion

According to *Megatrends for Women*, the 1992 work
authored by Patricia Aburdene and John Naisbitt, the new
breed of manager embraces an approach known as the
"Women's Leadership Style." "Consultants tried to teach
male managers to relinquish the command-and-control
mode. For women, it was different: it just came naturally.
This supportive style creates a 'think tank' like atmosphere."

*"When momma ain't happy,
ain't nobody happy!"*

—Southern saying

Here are some tips for working for a woman boss:

- **Use her nurturing nature to your advantage.** This
  is said to be a basic instinct in women. Accept the
  concept that your woman manager will beam when
  you succeed and she's able to say "and I helped!"
- **Make her look good.** This works for both genders,
  but remember that after reaching goals and
  successfully implementing initiatives, she'll most likely
  delight in sharing credit with all who deserve it. This

doesn't mean you can act like the reincarnation of Eddie Haskell—just genuinely work to make the group, as a whole, succeed.

- **Be clear about the type of mentoring you need.** While we all love having our egos stroked, reality kicks in and tells us that we need instructive input even more. Women adapt well to different styles if you just let them know your needs.

  > For example, I personally respond best to the coach who acts more as a "drill sergeant" and keeps me accountable. If the coach simply compliments me on how great I am, I tend to slack off and skate by. No output equals no growth, so if I see this happening, I take steps to steer the relationship back on track.

- **Tap into her network.** The Bad New Girls' Network (counterpart to the Good Old Boys' Network!) is getting stronger as the numbers of women in top management increase. My experience is that women enjoy seeing their protégées grow. So ask to be introduced to others whom your woman boss thinks would benefit from knowing you.

  Take the high road by paying back favors, volunteering your time, writing follow-up notes, etc. Oh, and keep your boss up to date about the relationships you are growing as a result of her introductions.

- **Keep your cool.** One stereotype is that women can be "overly emotional". Have you ever heard this comment?—"A woman could never be president because women are so emotional. She could be in a bad mood and push the button starting World War III!" Emotions and how we display them have nothing to do with hormones or gender. It is all about emotional maturity and intelligence. So, keep your emotions in check regardless of your boss's gender. Venting is fine, but save it for a confidant . . . or better yet, for your personal journal!

- **Don't interrupt.** While this may seem like common courtesy, women are generally better listeners than men. And men tend to interrupt more often than women. When listening, keep a mental list of things you want to discuss, or jot down one or two words as reminders. If she doesn't request input when she has finished, ask permission to give it. For example: "Laura, are you open to some feedback about the Peterman Proposal?" Of course, I am talking about one-on-one discussions here, not putting her in an embarrassing position in front of a group.

Working for a woman boss can provide you with a great foundation to learn and develop in your field. Invest time in creating the right attitude and open communication up-front. Ask her to clearly define expectations and measurements. You'll probably end up way ahead of your competition!

# The Boss From Hell—Make It A Learning Experience

What if your boss:

- Doesn't support your goals?
- Doesn't recognize your accomplishments?
- Verbally abuses you?
- Steals your ideas?

The number one factor in retaining quality employees is the manager. If employees are learning, being fairly compensated, having fun and feeling appreciated, they stick around. Today's team environment demands leaders with good communication skills who can motivate employees and provide stretch assignments.

## Stand Up to the Bully

One of my first jobs was in Washington, D.C. for what is now a major airline. I was excited about the opportunity, and the man who would be my boss was an older gentleman with a big smile, who had been with the firm for over 25 years. On my second day at work, I was on the phone talking with a customer when I noticed my boss step out of his office to watch me. As I ended the call, I said, "Yes, sir. I will follow up on your question and call you back within the hour." I looked up to see my wonderful boss scowling at me with a face as red as a beet. He screamed, "Don't you ever let me hear you talking on the phone in such a subservient way again! What are you, some kind of slave? If you can't step up to the responsibility of your position, you can just quit now. Don't you ever let me hear you say 'sir' or 'ma'am' in this office again."

Whoa! As the daughter of a career military officer and a polite, southern woman, I was raised to respect my elders. I was only 25 years old at this time, talking to an older man on the phone, having an even older man yell at me for being polite. Of course, I went to the bathroom and cried because I felt like a failure.

So what should you do when your boss is a jerk? Stand up to him. Remember the first time someone bullied you when you were a child? We quickly learn that showing fear and backing down brings on more abuse. So directly confront the person.

## Kill 'em with Kindness

I talked with my wise mother about it and reacted differently the next time. When he yelled at me, I simply smiled, nodded, and said, "Sure, Mr. Hayes, I appreciate your advice", and went about my work. After he did this a couple more times, I actually went into his office and said, "Mr. Hayes, you seem to be very stressed. Is there anything I can do to help out?" He was speechless! That was the last day he ever treated me rudely. In fact, he later became a terrific mentor.

## Three Tries and He's Out

Bottom line, we can control a lot of the verbal abuse simply by the way we react. Now let's make this clear: Do not put up with this type of conduct for long. Make the person aware of their behavior. Often, this type of person is not aware of what they are doing. Once they *are* made aware through your feedback, they must step up to the plate and accept responsibility to change. If there is no change, it's time to go to a third party for mediation.

I have seen several cases in my consulting practice where a high-level manager was forced to attend what I call "charm school." Temper tantrums, verbal abuse, management by fear and intimidation are out, so these folks will have to leave these traits behind.

## Don't Be a Victim

Raising awareness to your boss's bad behavior is the first step. If they do not choose to make changes, bring in a third party to mediate. Overall, everyone will benefit from this strategy. And the job will get done!

# Managing Your Manager

---

*"People with goals succeed because they know where they're going."*

— *Earl Nightingale*

---

There is nothing like having a great boss. In fact, retention studies show that having an enjoyable working relationship is the key reason employees remain with an organization.

When employees feel unappreciated, trapped, bored and restless, their natural response is to act exactly how the boss fears they will: They learn how to do just enough to get by. Before you know it, mediocrity, rather than excellence, is the standard.

## Take the Initiative

Many employees still see their company (and therefore, their boss) as a "parental" figure. But in reality, we drive our own careers. Take charge of establishing a mutually valuable relationship with your manager and you will *know* you are working toward getting what you need and want.

## Figure Out What's Important

- Find out exactly what is important to your boss

- Determine your boss's responsibilities
- Establish the goals for each area
- Ascertain how you can help accomplish those goals
- Make sure it happens

## Over-Communicate

- Check out the communication links in your organization and how your boss functions within them
- Learn each other's communication styles
- Spend some time getting to know one another
- Let your manager take the lead, but if nothing happens, take the initiative to ask for one-on-one time together

## Keep Your Boss Personally Updated

A common complaint is: "My boss has no idea what I *really* do." If your manager does not take control on this two-way street, you must step forward.

- Ask for a 20-minute meeting every two weeks or even once a week.
- Schedule the meeting in a conference room or other private setting where you can sit next to your boss, rather than across from him.
- Prepare your agenda items in advance. Your manager will appreciate your organizational skills and consideration of management's time constraints.

## Weekly Accomplishments

Keep a running list of your accomplishments in a convenient place—your computer, Day-Timer® or a spiral pad. By adding to the list every day, you will never forget what you have done. Submit this list to your manager for discussion during your face-to-face meetings.

In addition, keep a "Kudos File" in which you put all accomplishment lists, complimentary letters from customers, documentation of courses attended and other significant information. This file will prove invaluable at evaluation time — especially if you have a boss who tells you to write your own evaluation. You will never be at a loss for words!

## Ask for Mentoring

An article in the March 1999 issue of *Business Week* stated, "Data from the 1999 Energizing Workforce Study show that 35% of employees who don't receive regular mentoring plan to look for another job within 12 months. But just 16% with good mentors expect to jump ship." Both management and your boss are responsible for assuring your career development.

It is in *your* best interest to let your boss know what type of mentoring or development you need and want. Most bosses tend to avoid micromanaging when they know how to support their employees.

- Let your manager know that you desire a mentor
- Ask for opportunities to discuss your career objectives
- Provide suggestions for effective coaching tips applicable to *you*

## Let Your Boss Know Where You Are Headed

Ultimately, you are the one charting your path for future development. Decide exactly where you want to go . . . for *now*.

- Ask for classes or other means for you to grow. Obtaining academic certifications has never been easier.

- Ask for individual career development training. A recent Society for Human Resources Management (SHRM) survey showed that over 90% of organizations now offer training reimbursement programs in addition to company-sponsored course work.

## Create Learning Opportunities

- Make a list of opportunities for career development within your organization by observing and understanding the entire company operations.
- Volunteer to take on new assignments or participate on cross-functional teams.
- Keep your manager updated on your progress.
- Ask for chances to show what you can do and determine how these opportunities can be arranged.
- Investigate job openings available within the company or other possible jobs outside the company to develop your career goals.

## Keys to Advancement

The Center for Creative Leadership, headquartered in Greensboro, North Carolina, cites five key experiences that help employees develop and grow:

- Challenging jobs
- Interacting with other people, especially managers
- Hardships
- Course work
- Off-the-job experiences

Overall, take the stance that you want your boss to be not only a boss, but an advocate, mentor and coach. If you get a "lemon", don't run away. Excel—no matter how unhelpful your boss is—and you will learn and grow from the experience. Don't try to outmaneuver or outsmart your manager. Make yourself indispensable and then move toward your own goals.

Remember, no matter where you are on the organizational ladder, *you* have the power to transform your relationship with your boss. Don't lose it!

# When Is It Too Soon To Leave a Job? Your Six-Step Checklist

---

*"It's never to late to be what you might have been."*

— George Eliot

---

"*W*e're mad as hell and we're not going to take it anymore!" Remember that great line from the movie *Network*? That's right, no more Mr. Nice Guy. Now it is Me Inc. No more loyalty! I am going to look out for Number One, right? Well, sorta. And sorta not! With today's staffing model, we are all able to change jobs more frequently, experience more, build a broader network and generally make more money. But when is it **too soon** to leave one opportunity for another?

In the world of freelancers, e-lancers and contract workers, we frequently look at a job as an assignment, viable for a set period of time. Even if you are not a contract worker, the mentality is the same. Though we are all on our own when it comes to career development, jumping too soon from "assignment" to "assignment" can cause a ripple effect that can sully a reputation.

Think of your work in terms of what *your* expectations are. What do you really want to get out of it? And how long are you willing to wait for it? Let a company know those things up-front when you come on board.

For example, when I joined one firm, they wanted me to handle two functions simultaneously. I wasn't crazy about this idea, as I considered each one a full-time effort. I knew I would end up spending more time on the revenue-generating functions, while the administrative side would suffer. I felt that I could "cover the bases" handling both, but would the end results be there? So, I agreed to do it for one year and at the end of that time, would segue the tasks to others whom I had mentored. It worked beautifully; both the company and I got what we wanted. Consider the opposite scenario, though. If it hadn't worked out, it would have been considered a failure on my scorecard. So be sure you only take calculated risks when accepting stretch assignments!

When I begin to feel antsy while working on a specific project, I depend on my six-step checklist, which allows me to evaluate whether it is "too soon to leave." Your own checklist may contain more points, or fewer, with different criteria. Mine are:

- What was my initial commitment?
- What am I learning?
- Is my compensation up to par?
- Do I enjoy and am I thriving in the company's culture?
- Do I admire top management and buy in to their vision?
- Why am I considering leaving? Am I running from anything?

**What was my initial commitment?** When playing a key project role, many are depending on your commitment to make it work. Abandoning a project can result in lost revenues and customers. Agree up-front to the time commitment with contingencies for extensions built in. And never leave the organization in a bind. Give at least two weeks' notice when moving on, and offer to help locate and train a successor.

**What am I learning?** I have a high need to be in an upward learning curve at all times. I want to learn new industry trends, expand my network and be exposed to cutting-edge strategies. If this isn't a large part of the quotient, I lose interest fast and start seeking new territory. To maintain marketability, you have to take stretch assignments and experiment with your new skills.

**Is my compensation up to par?** By using the Internet and talking with others, I am able to keep up with industry compensation trends. Signing bonuses, perks, etc. are a part of the quotient when evaluating whether it is time to leave. Going to a new position is, without a doubt, a great way to get a raise.

**Am I thriving in the company's culture?** Because we spend over a third of our time and energy on our job, I think it is important to be very comfortable in the environment and with our coworkers. Are people friendly and optimistic? Do they feel a sense of pride in working for the organization? Does the firm perpetuate communication and an atmosphere of spirit and respect for the individual?

**Do I admire top management and buy in to their vision?** Management is more responsible than any other factor when it comes to employee morale and attitude. Do the "Powers That Be" embody traits and values aligned with my own? Do I truly believe in their projects/services and want them to succeed?

**Why am I considering leaving?** "Am I running from anything?" would be an important question to ask myself. At one position, I was very content until a new senior vice president came in and made my life miserable. Or so I felt. When I started looking around, I realized that every organization is dysfunctional in some way and that the prize is in learning to deal with these challenging people!

## Most Jobs Last 2-5 Years

Remember, in the world of rapidly changing work positions, we tend to cross paths with the same people more than once. The average job life is 2-5 years. Make sure your scorecard is perfect when you are being considered for a new opportunity and that your integrity and reputation are flawless. Follow my six-step formula and you will never have to look for an assignment again! People will come looking for *you*!

# CHAPTER NINE

*Shamelessly Marketing Your Talents*

# New Grads: What Companies Are Looking For

---

*"I'm a great believer in luck, and I find the harder I work the more I have of it."*

— *Thomas Jefferson*

---

$A$lthough launching a career might be exciting for some new graduates, the truth is that many feel overwhelmed at the daunting task of selling themselves to the world. And that is exactly what landing a job is—a *sales* process.

## The Sales Project

The job search process is best approached as a project. Its milestones include:

- **Assessing your skills and traits**
- **Creating your sales documents**
- **Conducting research**
- **Making sales presentations**
- **Closing the deal**

Start by thinking realistically about your beginning base salary. Multiply that figure by the number of years you would ideally like to remain at that position. The sum is the "price tag" on your "product". Say you would like to start at $35K and be at that position for three years. Your product is on the market for $105K.

Now that you have established your price, assess your key skills. Make a list of everything that makes you unique. Take time to know yourself and be able to express your strengths and weaknesses. This will distinguish you from the crowd.

## What Are Companies Buying?

Now take a look at what companies need and want. If you are selling skills and traits that have no value in today's marketplace, there won't be a match anytime soon. Here are inside tips on what employers look for. This list comes directly from the mouths of hiring managers, so listen up!

- **GPA** can be an important factor in the initial screening process. Quite a few organizations make their initial cut based on this. If your overall GPA is mediocre but better in your major, emphasize that. If it is not so great, remember that there has been no proven correlation between grades and work success. Instead, sell a prospective employer on your skills, traits, attitude and enthusiasm.
- **Communication skills** are needed today for *any* organization to succeed. Regardless of how basic this may seem, the number one ability preferred by employers is being able to communicate both verbally and in writing. If you haven't taken a public speaking course yet, sign up for Toastmasters, or register for a course at your local community college. It will pay off immeasurably. Your writing skills should be reasonably sharp at this time, but if not, check out a business writing course.

- **Interpersonal skills** are next on the list. Take those great communication skills to the next level. With teamwork being key to completing work, you should be able to relate to all kinds of people. A major part of candidate evaluation is based on the ability to relate and interact with company representatives and clients.

- **Multi-level relationships** are necessary to work successfully with your peers and managers. Many people you meet in the workplace may be less educated formally, but their years of experience give them a perspective from which you can learn. Are you able to take direction and follow through?

- **Leadership ability** is one of the most sought-after skills that graduates can possess at the beginning of their careers. Inventory all of your leadership experiences, including positions held in campus organizations, extracurricular activities and part-time jobs.

- **Enunciation and verbalization** are required to clearly articulate what you want. Otherwise, indecision will emerge during an interview. Focus on the industry, skills and roles you are interested in playing. This will differentiate you as being committed to a particular organization or industry, rather than someone who just needs a job to pay the rent.

- **Flexibility** will make you much more attractive to any employer. Are you willing to work non-traditional hours, move from one role to another, relocate, travel? The less rigidity you show, the more you will shine.

- **Character and integrity** were listed together in my informal survey. An employer wants a sense that you are honest, have a strong value system and can be trusted. You know what needs to be done and you do it right, on time, and without reminders or supervision.

- **Reliability and steadfastness** are signs of maturity. Do you have your act together? Are you able to either deal with issues or ask for help in resolving them? Do you have reliable transportation? And by the way, the more you keep your personal life to yourself, the better off you will be.
- **Initiative and enthusiasm** must be demonstrated and documented in a manner that highlights the value you add. Let your employer know that you realize working with them provides you opportunities to make or save money for the firm. Suggest ways to function more effectively as well.

You will come out way ahead by demonstrating that you possess these traits and skills, along with a positive attitude. Be prepared to communicate examples of your skills and the ways you can contribute to an organization.

Remember — you are selling your ability to help *them* reach *their* goals. This strategy will lead you to your perfect position. Once you land it, remember that the one thing that separates successful people from those who are not is their willingness to work very, very hard!

# College Grads—
# Landing Your First Job

---

*"Choose a job you love and you will never*
*work a day in your life."*

— *Confucius*

---

Whoopee, graduate! You made it! It's your turn to go out and make your mark on the world. And there's good news! According to the National Association of Colleges and Employers (NACE), companies are forecasting a nearly 15% increase in the number of job opportunities. Many are hiring new grads, as organizations can neither find nor afford more experienced candidates.

## What are Your Potential Obstacles?

When asked their biggest obstacle in finding that dream job, a third of all graduates stated "competition". Other key reasons were a mediocre GPA and just not knowing how to conduct a job search. Each is just a speed bump in your road to success. Now is the time to start getting your act together so you can take it on the road! Your secret weapons will be **initiative**, **enthusiasm** and **flexibility**.

Most new grads don't have a realistic view of what is needed to land a great position. In fact, quite a few think that:

- They are skilled, fresh and smart
- A company will come and find them
- A job will fall from heaven, like manna

In reality, you've got to be proactive to stand out from the crowd.

## Hiring Trend

The hiring trend is shifting away from on-campus interviewing. According to NACE, only 5% of on-campus interviews result in an actual job. So start looking beyond the campus and great possibilities will surface. Career management, along with the continuous search for terrific work, is a life skill you will forever develop. Think of your first professional job search as laying the cornerstone to your career's foundation.

## Uncover Your Fit

Focus on your exceptional skills. What talents do you most enjoy? If you look at the long term—the big picture—you will most likely discover where you really belong after you have tried numerous positions. It is a process of elimination, trying different industries, and various sized organizations and cultures. Don't worry about the long term at this point—just decide what is best for **now**.

I can remember feeling the pressure of accepting the *right* position and finding the *right* organizations. Who needs that kind of pressure? Accept something that is appealing and takes you toward your overall goals.

# Your Sales Brochure

You need a top-notch resume. Think of it as your "sales brochure". Do **not** create a different resume for each position. You will be much better off with one document that outlines your unique talents and accomplishments. Then customize your cover letter to fit a specific position.

Dozens of effective resume formats are available online. Make it a goal to create a document that is concise, error-free, in a 10 — to 12-point font, and on white or cream-colored paper. You want to stand out, but unless you're a candidate for a position requiring creativity, such as graphic arts, stick to classic formats and stationery.

Begin with your overall *Objective*. Keep it generic. The standard "Seeking an entry-level position with a growth-oriented firm that utilizes my skills" is simply not going to cut it. Instead, try listing your area of expertise, such as "Information Technology" or "Accounting". Let a potential employer help figure out where you fit, instead of eliminating you because you have a narrow objective.

Remember to list any experience that shows your ability to complete a job. Summer jobs, internships and volunteer work are all relevant. The object is to show your uniqueness.

# Interviewing

Go into the interview with the attitude that you are looking for common ground. If there is none, it is still a terrific experience and you will meet some new contacts. You have about five seconds to make your first impression, so make it "as good as it gets". Walk in with a big smile, a warm, friendly attitude, and a confident handshake. Be yourself. Don't risk selling false expectations that you will have to live up to every day if they hire you!

The tools of the trade include a quality "interview suit".

Navy blue is still the favorite for both male and female, but more importantly, you should be neat and well-tailored. If you can, keep the piercings, tattoos and spiked hair under wraps.

## Personal Mission Statement

A question that you may hear when interviewing goes something like "What is your personal mission statement?" This is information that new grads often do not yet have a clue about. So, focus on **now**.

- What are your goals within the next few years?
- Will you be working toward a higher level of certification in your chosen field?
- Is your key goal to get some basic experience under your belt?
- Do you want to get your foot in the door at a specific company?

When addressing the mission statement question, keep it general and be open to shifting your focus if your research shows the market is not buying what you are selling. Be honest. For instance: "I am in a learning mode and want to work in an environment where I can make a contribution and have stretch assignments".

## Research

Even if your interview is for a part-time cashier at the local fast-food hangout, spend a couple of hours researching in advance. Check out their corporate Web site.

- What new strategies are being implemented?
- Do they have any new products?
- What does their target customer look like?
- What values and goals does the company stand for?

Talking about *their* needs will make *your* stock value go way up. If you walk in with a folder of information, the focus is on how your skills fit in with their needs, instead of the fact that you need a job so you can afford your car payment and rent.

## Be Patient and Proactive

Approaching work as an adventure and as a life-long pursuit will uncover positions to expand both your experience and skills. Consider your first few positions as "paying your dues" and learning the rules of business life.

While work serves different purposes for us all, I maintain that if you choose something that is fun for you, you *will* succeed! Believe it and you will live it!

# The Job Search As A Project

---

*"Start by doing what's necessary,*
*then do what's possible, and suddenly,*
*you are doing the impossible.*

— *Saint Francis of Assisi*

---

Been in the job market lately? Thinking of entering it sometime soon? If you haven't already begun the job search process, then now is the perfect time to start! If you think it's okay to start looking for a new job only when you *need* one, think again. You need to make an adjustment and begin the continual process of managing your career!

Although the job market fluctuates, the new rules of work demand that we be in the perpetual mode of searching for new projects to increase skills, satisfaction and salary. If you consider your job search a project, dividing it into steps, you will be much more organized.

## Identify Goals

As you identify your goals, make the following assessments:

- What type of work are you seeking? Industry? Company size? What skills will you be using?

- What kind of compensation do you expect? List all the items for which you want to negotiate, from base salary, to number of days off, to job title.
- When do you want to begin your new position?

Write down all of your goals and adjust them as you progress.

## Resources

- The term "resources" can mean many things, but as you take stock of your resources, consider these items:
- **Tangibles.** Do you have a computer, fax machine and reliable voice mail?
- **Budget.** How long can you "afford" to be without an income? A reduced income?
- **People.** Who do you know that you can talk to about your goals, for referrals and ideas?
- **Community.** Does yours have job transition centers that offer support and courses?
- **Industry.** In what professional organizations are you active?

## Tools

When you are clear about your goals, your marketing materials will reflect accomplishments supporting them. Your resume and cover letters will represent you in the competitive marketplace, so take time to ensure they are topnotch. Get a professional opinion and ask the readers to give you feedback on what they think you are "selling" in terms of skills and abilities. Sometimes we emphasize the wrong things.

   **Hint:** Invest in some business cards. You can order them from office supply stores, over the Internet and at copy centers. You do not need a company name and title. Simply list your name and contact information. If you want, you can list areas of expertise such as "Information Technology Specialist". Leave your cards behind after interviews, give them to network contacts and exchange them at meetings.

## Benchmarks—Measurements

- Part of successfully managing a project means setting milestones and measurements to make sure you stay on track. In managing your job search project, try these tips for creating benchmarks:
- Figure that you will need to talk to about 25 hiring managers to land your position. This means that you will need to keep accurate records about which companies you contact, along with details of the exchange.
- Plan the number of contacts you will make each week and stick to your goal. Try to maintain contact with 10 new sources weekly. It often takes several attempts to reach your contacts. By setting a reasonable number, you will stay on top of things.

## Record-keeping

- **Create records that fit your style.** If you love your PalmPilotÒ, then use it for your records. If you are a visual person, use 3x5 cards or notebooks with your files. Another effective method is to set up a portable file case containing all relevant materials.
- **Keep copies of everything.** Retain a copy of every letter, phone discussion notes, etc. for each prospect. Once you are rolling, the process will snowball and it will be difficult to remember details without your notes!

# Follow-up

A secret tactic of successful job seekers is follow-up. Anyone can make initial contact, but the individuals who follow up and keep themselves in the minds of hiring managers more often get the call back. Increase your chances for a call using these tips:

- Keep in mind that you are looking for information during this process. If there is no "job" available, keep in touch and let people know where you are in your search.
- "It ain't over till it's over". If you uncover an opening or interesting opportunity and aren't selected for it, remain in contact every 3-4 months. You never know when something just right for you will evolve.

# Take Action!

When you know where you are headed, your network is current, your skills are in demand and your outlook is positive, the opportunities will continue to appear. "Begin difficult things while they are easy . . . a thousand-mile journey begins with one step," said Lao Tse. Take a step today—your timing is perfect!

# Three Steps To Finding Your Perfect Job

---

*"The majority work to make a living; some work to acquire wealth or fame, while a few work because there is something within them which demands expression."*

— *Edmond Boreaux Szekely*

---

Finding your "perfect job" is a life-long process. To find the perfect job means to create your *own* nirvana. That is, honing and building your skills over the years until you find the environment, industry, mission and skills match that fit together as your perfect combination. To achieve this, you must sometimes be willing to step back in order to move forward. My belief is that we spend more time planning our vacations than our careers.

## Common Problem with Careers

I have been fortunate over the past 10 years to be able to strategize career directions with people of all ages, skill groups, income levels and cultures. One expression of frustration I hear consistently is: "My problem is that I don't know what I want to be when I grow up." I recommend that you start your career discovery process with the premise that you never have to *be* something. Be a combination of your motivated skills — the ones you do effortlessly and enjoy learning more about.

## Blend Your Career from Motivated Skills

My own path has gone from being a waitress, to teaching German, to co-owning a restaurant in Germany, to working in international business, to coaching others on international careers, to consulting, training and speaking. I started out in the educational mode and still work in that general area part of the time. But the business skills I have picked up along the way provide me with a wide vista, rather than tunnel vision, when helping others.

I continue to rely on my facilitation, business, people, international and consulting skills in many arenas, not just one. This not only keeps my interest up, but also allows me to consistently evolve into new niches and experience many work situations. Yes, I could have continued to teach at the same school where I started. In fact, some of my friends who remained there are eligible for retirement in several years. But what a tradeoff!

## Step One—Take Stock

If you are willing to "do the work", you too can create your perfect scenario. Begin by taking an inventory of your best skills *and* the ones you enjoy the most. Your second inventory will consist of things you enjoy in your personal time, as well as your work time. What are your favorite activities? What would you spend time doing if money were not a consideration?

While this exercise may sound simple, many people are unable to overcome their own roadblocks to carry out this creative thinking process. For instance, they think they are too old to start over, don't have the right education, or would have to take a cut in pay. People who morph their careers and build on their interests will attest that it all evens out. In fact, those who follow their dreams usually end up ahead in every sense of the word, as their work and play overlap into a lifestyle.

## Step Two—Do Research

During this stage, you will be researching companies, industries and needs. Create a list of organizations you have heard are dynamic places to work. Talk with friends who know both your talents and style. Ask them what they see as key skills and traits that make you unique.

Brainstorm with your friends to discover where your skills would be an asset. After each discussion, add new ideas to your master list. Soon, you will have a huge list of ideas. The more outrageous the ideas, the more you will realize how deeply you have been blocked by your own limitations.

## Step Three—Begin to Volunteer

This critical step is the place where most fall out because they don't want to "do the work". When you get involved with things on a voluntary basis, others see you thrive and they begin to trust in your skills. When I started my international business career, I already had a rich background in personal experiences, as I had traveled and lived abroad. However, I had no business experience; therefore, I had no credibility in the business world.

After doing some research, I discovered that a lot of the movers and shakers met at a monthly World Trade Association meeting. I called and volunteered to work at the next meeting and was consequently asked to sit at the registration table and write name tags. This afforded me the opportunity, as a newcomer, to meet every member as they signed in. Within three years, I was the first-ever woman president of this 675-member organization.

Volunteering is key, as it helps you build credibility and contacts, as well as gain a realistic view of working in a particular industry. It affords you the opportunity to meet people who are willing to talk openly about their jobs, how they got them, and their pros and cons. And, most importantly, you will learn whether or not the work is something you would like to pursue on a full-time basis.

## Success Story

A successful attorney I worked with had been laid off from his corporate position after 18 years. While he was very competent at law, he no longer enjoyed it. So he made a list of his key skills and motivators, including some thoughts about how he liked to spend his time.

He began to talk to business colleagues and friends about his career path. Through this process, he realized that he had always wanted to be a professor. He began to speak at local universities as a subject matter expert and within six months, was a full-time professor at a business school. By combining his legal and corporate expertise with his love of the academic environment, he was able to find his ideal position. As an instructor, his new mission involved the good feeling that results from helping others to develop, rather than the tension that so often accompanies lawsuits.

Remember — successful people do things on a continual basis that unsuccessful people neglect to do. In other words, step back, reassess and do the work to discover what makes you tick. The rewards will be unlimited. If you find what you love to do, you will never work another day in your life!

# Interviewing—It's A Sales Call!

---

*"Enthusiasm releases the drive to carry you over obstacles and adds significance to all you do."*

— *Normal Vincent Peale*

---

You finally did it: You landed an interview for the job of your dreams. Tomorrow is the big day and you're as cool as a cucumber. Why? Because you are approaching the meeting as a sales call, not an interrogation.

The best approach to interviewing is really about assessing the needs of the organization, as well as the skills and goals of the applicant, to determine whether or not there is a match. If there is, the discussion continues. If not, you have made a new contact and may be able to direct another candidate to the company.

## Assess Needs

Before your interview, plan to spend quite a bit of time researching. Act just like a detective gathering information and getting the lay of the land in advance.

If possible, check out the company's place of business. Don't get nutty and act like a stalker—just spend a few minutes in the parking lot around lunchtime. You will be able to observe how employees interact with one another and get an idea of their typical dress, as well as the pace of the organization. Do people look happy, or are they speeding out of the building and parking lot, looking stressed? If no one comes out, that can be a red flag, too: They may be so overloaded with work, they can't even take a lunch break!

Using your networking skills, make calls to some people you know and tell them that you are interested in the company. Ask them if they have heard anything about the firm—on or off the record. Do they have any friends or contacts working there? Make as many casual calls as possible to find out about the culture, tone, and attitude of the organization. What skills are in highest demand at this time? What about the available position? Why is it open? What is the personality or management style of the person to whom you will directly report?

Of course, you should also study the company's Web site to get a flavor for their products, image, organizational makeup, etc. We all know, however, that the projected public image and actual experience at the company are two totally different things. But your work and research will really pay off in the long run.

## Know the Value of Your Skills

Before heading to the interview, research salary surveys to put a dollar figure on your skills. You do not want to discuss compensation until an offer has been made, but knowing your range up-front is part of your sleuthing. Companies often create positions to fit the skills a talented candidate brings to the table. If asked what salary range you are seeking, request to defer the discussion until you know more about the responsibilities and requirements of the job.

# Sell Yourself

Now here is where your research will pay off. You have the liberty of asking lots of questions about the position:

- What does the ideal candidate "look like"?
- What key skills is the employer seeking?
- What are the critical tasks for the first six months?
- What resources are available?
- What is the main goal for the position?

Point out past accomplishments similar to their current needs. Let them know how your skills can immediately meet their requirements and help them reach their goals. You are the solution to their problem.

## Close the Sale

As the question-and-answer portion of the interview winds down, be proactive in closing your sale. Ask for the job! If the interviewer says something like "Thanks for your time today; we will be in touch", ask what the next steps are. Inquire about the time frame for their decision. And, most importantly, ferret out any potential objections to their hiring you, and underscore your strengths. It will show your honest interest in their feedback and requirements.

As you leave, if you're feeling positive about the match, *tell the interviewer,* and come right out and ask for the position. Let them know that you have taken time to assess the fit you are looking for, and that you are enthusiastic about the prospect of working together. Make it clear that you have a keen interest in partnering with them to help successfully tackle their projects.

# Follow-Up . . . Follow-Up . . . Follow-Up

The last step is where so many candidates fall off the short list. While great follow-up won't land you the job if you aren't a top candidate, it can be a tiebreaker. Write short, handwritten letters to each person involved in your interviewing process. Reinforce the strengths and accomplishments you can bring to the organization. Focus on the skills they really need. And again, ask for the job. Remember, they have no idea how many offers you have pending or if they are at the top of your list, unless you tell them.

Follow the simple method of putting the organization's needs ahead of your personal focus during the interview process. The result will be job offers that meet *your* goals, too!

# Surviving The Restaurant Interview

---

---

Eating is one thing that most of us seem to do on a daily basis . . . and yet many of my clients feel uncomfortable when being interviewed in a restaurant setting. It seems that table manners and protocol are almost an "old fashioned" topic that many of today's workers are unfamiliar with. While some of us will never have to worry about having good enough table manners to feel comfortable eating at the White House, a little bit of knowledge can set you apart from your competition in a heartbeat!

Here are some points to consider before you show up at your next restaurant interview. Just having an awareness of these basics can boost your confidence level.

- Take the view that eating is the secondary agenda of the meeting. I even recommend that you don't arrive hungry! Especially if you are typically a person who experiences stomach growling, light-headedness or any other reaction when you don't eat at your regular time. Eat a small snack such as an apple or protein bar about an hour before your meeting to prevent these reactions in the event the eating part of the meal is delayed.

- Arrive with as little as possible — Leave the briefcase, pager and cell phone in the trunk of your car. Do bring along your portfolio with paper, pen and a couple of resumes.
- Treat everyone with equal respect. We all know the person who acts as if the busboy or server is several notches lower on the social ladder. This type of behavior sends a message of arrogance that is not tolerated by many.
- When ordering your beverage, refrain from alcohol. Not only can it hinder your concentration; you never know how the interviewer feels about the subject. They might just be ordering alcohol to observe what *you* do! If the interviewer orders alcohol, you can also play it safe by following their lead and ordering it as well, but just taking a sip or two.
- If you live in an area that still allows smoking in restaurants, it is still better to refrain and go for the "Non-smoking Section" if asked.
- If there are already beverages such as water on the table when you sit down, your is the one to your *right* — above your knife and spoon.
- The napkin is customarily put in your lap as soon as you sit down rather than waiting until your food actually arrives.
- The best beverages to order are those without carbonation, strong color or odor. You don't need to be burping cola. Or wiping spilled coffee off of your new interview jacket. Tea and water are easier.
- The small plate on your left is for bread. If you use your knife to butter the bread, rest the knife on the bread plate rather than putting it back on the table.

- When ordering, take a look at the menu and be done with it. If you spend ten minutes trying to decide what you want, a mixed signal is sent out. I would be wondering . . . hmmm, how long does it take this person to prioritize their work if it takes them this long to pick out a lunch order? Will they freeze up when required to make decisions bigger than what to eat?
- Order something that does not need to be eaten with your hands or require excessive cutting. For example, casseroles or salads basically require your fork only. Pastas are a good choice too as they can be cut with your fork. Avoid long pastas such as spaghetti and linguini that can fly off your fork even when twisted. If you have to pick the food up, there is a risk of the contents spilling out — maybe even on you.
- Don't do substitutions! We all know the person who asks for ingredients to be left out, want to change all the side orders and needs all the sauces and dressings "on the side". While I am not against ordering your food as you like it in a restaurant, the idea here is to be low maintenance. Order something simple and leave it at that.
- Use utensils beginning from the outside and working inward. For example, if you are eating a salad, use the fork on the far outside left. The second fork is for your entrée.
- When your food arrives, it is customary to wait until everyone is served before you begin eating. The only exception is if someone orders an appetizer — which is eaten *prior* to the entrees arriving.
- Now, what to do with those arms? Keep your hands in your lap, on the chair arms, or rest your elbows or wrists on the table *until* the food arrives. At this point, keep those elbows and forearms off the table!

- When your food arrives, try eating a little bit before adding salt, pepper, hot sauce, whatever. The old theory is that if you make a judgment about the taste of the food before you even *try* it, you might also prejudge people, ideas . . . you get the drift!
- The waiter will not have to ask you if you are finished if you leave the international signal called "boating your oars.". Take both utensils — fork and knife — and lay them parallel across the middle of your plate. The server will then know you are ready for them to remove it.
- Some restaurants set a coffee cup in advance and bring coffee around at the end of a meal. Typically, the cup is upside down on the saucer. If you want some, simply turn your cup right side up and the server will know to fill it.
- Gals, if you think your lipstick needs refreshing after eating, you are going to have to tough it out. Resist pulling that lipstick out at the table.
- Allow your host to take care of the bill. When leaving, thank them for the meal. Even though it was their idea, it never hurts to acknowledge hospitality.

Read this over before your next luncheon interview or business meeting. Just focus on the meeting and keep the eating as the secondary event. You will make a positive impression — I guarantee it!

# Post-Interview Etiquette—
# Your Competitive Edge

---

*"My stance is that good manners will never
go out of style, and will, in fact, give you a leg
up over your competition."*

*— Camille Primm*

---

The business world is becoming more informal in every way. We are living in a "Me Society" and competition for the best jobs continues to be on the upswing, as we each attempt to stake out our territory and get noticed. With so much ambiguity, some of us are just plain confused about current etiquette. My stance is that good manners will *never* go out of style, and will, in fact, give you a leg up over your competition.

## What Do Most People Do?

The fact is that most people look at the job search as a chore and take no steps to stand out or be creative. They focus on getting the interview and then waiting to see if they are selected. In fact, this is what approximately 80% of candidates do after a big interview. The follow-up steps are actually quite important and will set you apart from the crowd. View the time *after* meeting about a position as time to *close the sale* of your skills.

## Before Leaving the Premises

As you finish your interview, inquire about the next steps from your key contact. By asking, you will know the exact protocol, which will take the guesswork out of the process. Ask if there is any reason for you not to be in the final group of candidates. Do you lack particular skills or traits they are seeking?

Next, make absolutely sure that you have the correct spelling of each person's name, as well as their title. You will be following up with each one individually.

Several years ago, I appeared for an interview prepared to meet with two parties. As it turned out, a panel of five conducted the interview. While people introduced themselves at the onset, there wasn't a comfortable means for me to confirm specific contact information during the session. When the host walked me to the lobby to pick up the next candidate, I simply lagged behind at the desk. I enlisted the support of the receptionist, who gave me complete details. In addition, she threw in several helpful comments about the selection process.

## Within 24 Hours

Phone? Fax? E-mail? Letter? What is the best method for keeping in touch with the interviewers? Of course, the answer is all of the above. Remember when you asked your key contact for the next steps? Follow that guidance first and foremost — and think of your response to the interview as your opportunity to reiterate what went right and recover from anything that may have fallen short of your expectations.

A **letter** is the most impressive form of follow-up. It takes more effort than the other options but can set you apart from the crowd. My recommendation is to hand write the correspondence if at all possible. If you're writing is atrocious, stick to the computer. But it is the one way the reader knows you are writing something unique, just for them, rather than sending the same letter with a different heading to each interviewer. A handwritten letter will catch their attention the minute it hits their desk.

Include your interest in their position and your key strengths. Reinforce your value with any additional thoughts you may have about the topics discussed.

Close with a statement that you are looking forward to the opportunity to partner with them in reaching their critical goals. Do not reinforce how much they will need *you*. It is all about what you have to offer to *them* — not how great you are.

**E-mails, faxes, and phone messages** are fine and definitely better than no follow-up at all. They just won't create the same impression. They are generally briefer and don't show the professional image that a letter does. I suggest relying on these forms *after* your initial, formal follow-up.

"How often can I call?" Many are unsure about the answer to this question. A good tactic is to leave a quick message stating that you are calling to check on the status of the position once a week. Don't ask them to call you back; they know you want to hear from them, and pushing the issue can get irritating. There is a very fine line between being a pest and being persistent — don't cross it!

## Recouping from Rejection

If you get the dreaded rejection letter, remember that the connection can still prove to be positive. When you receive a rejection, it is time to get out the stationery and write yet another follow-up. Express your positive impression of the organization and wish them continued success. Ask them to keep you in mind when the next opportunity arises.

Next, keep in touch with your key contact about once a month. If you see an article about the industry or a topic you discussed, forward it to the person with a short, handwritten note attached. Firms often create positions for *great* candidates — and you want to be in that category. They may even end up recommending you to a hiring manager at another firm.

Remember — follow-up is your closing opportunity to sell your skills. By creating the impression of attention to detail, professionalism and above all, good manners, you just can't go wrong!

# Getting To Know An Organization
## *Before* You Hop On Board

---

*"The achievements of an organization
are the results of the combined effort
of each individual."*

— *Vince Lombardi*

---

You are excited about starting a new position and can't wait
to dig into the work. The team and firm are so positive, and
you heard somewhere that they are employee-friendly. Plus,
the overtime will be great for getting ahead on the bills.

Fast-forward six months. You can't believe that you
didn't pick up on the fact that overtime meant "no life" at
this organization. Sure, the cash is great, but who has time
to spend it? And the smiles plastered on everyone's faces
during the interview are frozen into stressed, plastic masks.
What went wrong here?

A little investigative research could have avoided this situation.
Try these ideas to check out a firm before you are a member of the
team. Take off your rose-colored glasses and observe!

## Sleuthing

Put aside your own biases and open your mind to the

opinions of others. Rather than trying to get information to support your opinions at the onset, look for themes from more than one person—you may end up with a new attitude!

- **The company Web site** is one of the first faces presented to the outside world. Print out the pages and make notes:

    o  What image, mission, vision, values and goals
       are projected?
    o  Can you identify the tone of the materials?
    o  Does the information stress a pride in their
       people, products and services?
    o  What is the overall "feel" of the site?

- **Pay attention.** Last year, I met with one of the world's most progressive Fortune 100 companies to discuss a consulting assignment. When surfing the net for recent articles, I noticed that their CEO was featured on the cover of a just-released business publication. So, I stopped by the newsstand and picked up two copies. I read the piece thoroughly and learned some interesting details about the company's philosophy and talent.

    As a result, I was in a much better position during the interviewing process. I was able to emphasize their mission and how I could be a part of helping them meet their initiatives.

    I also took the magazine along and pulled it out during my discussion with the VP of human resources. He had not seen the article and was even unaware of the newly announced programs. He appreciated the copy I gave him, and I learned a priceless tidbit about communication within the organization.

**Ask your contacts** if they know anyone who works there or has worked there. Get their opinions on the atmosphere:

- What is your reporting manager's style?
- What is the overall culture of the organization — fast-paced, highly competitive, family owned?

Details straight from the source provide insights never gleaned by reading.

**Call trusted industry suppliers** with whom you have relationships and ask them about the company?

- Do they supply the company you are researching?
- Does the company pay their bills?
- Are the employees happy?
- What is the word on the street about their industry reputation?

**Make an advance drive-by.** Most organizations have some type of campus and lobby. Dress appropriately, drive over, park and watch people coming and going. Do they seem happy? Are they chatting in groups or do they seem to be isolated? Go inside the lobby and take a look around at the exhibits and awards inevitably displayed. Pick up any available literature — annual reports or product brochures.

One organization I encountered required visitors to walk a long distance from the parking area to a well-hidden doorway. So many employees had been laid off, I then had to use a speakerphone to call the person I was scheduled to meet. First, I had to look up their name on a keypad, which took another several minutes. By the time I actually got in, I had lost interest in the organization . . . way too impersonal for me!

The *Reader's Guide to Periodical Literature in*

*Business* is an invaluable resource and can be found in any library. It will lead you to recent articles about any organization. If you have access to a computer, the resources are endless. Reading what others have to say about the company is a terrific process.

- Is there a tone of respect for the organization?
- Does the media describe them as a leader in development, a model corporate citizen or the defendant in multiple lawsuits?
- **Dun's Business Rankings** provide accurate information about leading U.S. private and public businesses, having been a leader in this regard for some time. You can research by Standard Industrial Classification (SIC) code, state, size, etc., print out relevant details and add them to your catalogue of knowledge.
- **Hoover's Handbook of American Business** gives a comprehensive profile of over 500 American corporations. The data includes earnings, history and even a list of major competitors.
- **Poll recruiters and agencies.** There may be a disconnect between the inside story versus the organization's public face. Dig around and see what the industry professionals have to say about the firm. Have they placed clients in the organization or do they get a steady stream of new recruits from employees who are dying to get out of there?
- Call the local **Better Business Bureau** and inquire as to whether there are any outstanding complaints against the organization—multiple or class action suits.
- **Professional organizations** are generally made up of representatives from nearly all companies and offer a terrific forum for asking questions. You should be able to find someone who knows someone else who works there—from there, get the *rest* of the story!

Today's information age offers many advantages. Use them to get the real scoop before jumping on a company's bandwagon. Your research will pay off tenfold!

# Hiring Rates Rise As Temperatures Drop

---

*"Between saying and doing many*
*a pair of shoes is worn out."*

— *Italian Proverb*

---

When holiday seasons arrive, it may appear as though companies are just marking time during the last weeks of the year. In reality, this is one of the busiest times of the year for many organizations as they compete for top talent. The holiday season marks one of the prime hiring times to gear up for the upcoming year.

A decade ago, many firms tended to slow down during the holiday season and did not typically bring new employees on board during that time. Let's take a look at several reasons driving this change.

## New Breed of Workers

The layoff, reengineering, merging, reorganizing, de-installing, pink-slipping decade is taking its toll. When the psychological contract of "guaranteed employment" from a parental organization disappeared, so did worker loyalty. The mentality of "Me, Inc."—every worker for himself—

began to prevail, and firms experienced a backlash from their employee cutbacks. Talent is now a commodity on the market and free agents move from firm to firm depending on who has the best deal in the short term.

## Emphasis on Customer Service

New technology means shorter response time and a higher emphasis on providing exceptional customer service to both internal and external customers. Businesses that once operated on a 40-hour workweek are now running 24/7. This means that the search for qualified, skilled workers is never-ending. And the expectation for instant service is still on the rise.

## Headcount—Use It or Lose It

Operating budgets are tight and when additional headcount is approved, open personnel requisitions must often be filled by the end of the calendar year. Excess funds generally go back into the corporate pot for reallocation. For this reason, the pressure is often on during the last quarter to find just the right employee to fill the bill as time runs out.

## What the Experts Have to Say

When polling several Human Resource professionals for their perspective on hiring during the holidays, I got resoundingly similar feedback from each of them.

Louis Song, of Romac International, San Diego, stated that November and December are, in his experience, the busiest staffing months of the year. This year, like most others, show a rapid pace of hiring. "As companies spend out their budgets, they are preparing for the continued surge of E-Commerce development." This means staffing up *now* to have people in place.

Laurie Plachek, Human Resources Manager of Cox Communications, San Diego, says that the holidays and where they fall does not affect Cox's pace of recruiting and staffing. "We work 24/7 to provide services to our customers, so the time of year does not impact our hiring efforts."

"Staffing at this time of year can be challenging", said Judy Enns, PhD, Managing Director of HR Solutions, San Diego. Many workers do not want to make a significant change—particularly when involving relocation—during the holiday season. Often, they delay making their decisions, which has an impact on budgets and production." If anything", says Judy, "companies often work even harder to staff up during this time of year."

The big lesson here may be for job *seekers*—competition for jobs during this time is at an all time low . . . and companies have an all time demand. Firms may need to remember to be lenient with time off for newly signed employees where possible. It's a great time to create win-wins for both sides of table and enter a new year as a *team!*

# Get Noticed! Fuel Your Projects With Creativity

---

*"The chief enemy of creativity is "good" sense."*

— *Pablo Picasso*

---

Attention, competent professionals: The best projects don't always go to the most competent people—they often go to people who excel at marketing themselves and their contributions. It is no longer enough to be a whiz-bang programmer, research scientist or controller. Today's competition commands constant improvement in the processes around you, which means a hefty dose of creativity is needed. The good news is that innovation is an acquired skill. Not only can you learn how to be more creative, it can be fun and energizing as well.

## Assemble Your Team

The first step is getting the right people. Individuals who are enthusiastic about the project will be the most creative members of the team—they are willing to take more risks and learn by making mistakes. This also requires that they check their egos at the door and give up "right of ownership" on past projects.

## Out with the Old

Creation requires a certain amount of destruction—tearing down of the past and rebuilding into a new form. A successful project is composed of several great ideas built on top of one another. If your idea worked in the past, you must be willing to see it change and evolve as the project emerges—and to give credit to the team as a whole. Accept ideas from anyone, anywhere.

## Build a Creative Space

"War Rooms", as they are called are great creative spaces. They contain copies of all communications on a project. The project mission is posted on the wall on huge sheets of paper, and toys, such as Slinkysä, Play-Dohä and Smurf ä basketball hoops, are plentiful. Beverages and snacks are always on hand.

I like to set up a large space for Post-itä notes. I divide this area into sections and label them "Bright Ideas", "Kudos", "Lessons Learned" and "Need to Change." Team members can then post notes on the board at any time, and we address them in our next group meeting. The notes are then catalogued in a binder, along with the outcome from discussions, so team members who were not present can stay informed.

## Chart it Up

Set up an all-hands idea session at the onset of the project. Get impractical in your brainstorming and come up with virtually any solution to the tasks you face—no matter how wacky. This type of "green-light" thinking will stimulate creativity. Do some mental imaging. What will the outcome of the project "look like" — happy customers, more profits, a new product rolled out?

## Set Benchmarks

The next step is to break your project down into tasks and benchmarks and then divide your team into groups for each task. Using flip chart paper, each small task force draws what their outcome will look like and outlines the necessary steps to accomplish it. Then they present it to the group by posting it on the board, so everyone can add to it.

By having a visual concept of the project, steps and outcomes, each team member works toward a common goal that is clear and fully supports the mission. This technique can have terrific outcomes and provide a safe environment for team members to take subsequent assignments.

Anna Freud once said, "Creative minds always have been known to survive any kind of bad training". I agree that she was right on target! Provide a fun, open work environment by modeling that behavior yourself. I guarantee that you will be impressed with the outcome — and so will others!

# Promoting Your Skills At Work

---

---

You're a champ—and you know it. You always go the extra mile, take the high road and exceed expectations. Trouble is, someone else always seems to come out smelling like a rose by taking credit for your work. Or, you are always the one in the background because you think you are "just doin' your job." Time for a reality check!

Get ready to learn how to step up and take credit for your accomplishments. It's time to learn how to promote yourself at work.

## We're Programmed to be Modest

Most of us were raised to be modest and invisible within a group:

- Don't toot your own horn.
- Always just say "thank you" when someone compliments you.
- Never call attention to yourself by bragging.

These were some of the typical programming instructions heard by females in particular. If you take that track in the work environment today, you will be left in the dust!

## Self-Promotion Lessons Learned

Through many years of working in diverse environments, I have seen the whole range of self-promotion techniques. For instance, when working as a consultant on a project merging two huge organizations, I observed employees at all levels posturing and positioning to protect their territory. Some methods worked and others made people look glaringly ridiculous. Below are my picks for best practices on showcasing your skills.

## Spend Time Building Rapport

Rapport isn't just about being liked; it is also about creating a mutually beneficial sense of trust and attention for another person and their opinions. You are actually there to support each other in reaching personal goals. These days, the trend goes too far in focusing on the "Me, Inc." idea and not on teaming with others.

By the way, you do not have to *like* someone to gain rapport or to work productively together. Let go of your personal opinions and start asking them questions. Learn what makes them tick. When you take time to understand and really tune in to a person, rather than judge them, rapport naturally follows.

## Get Good at Self-Marketing

- Start out by "making a list and checking it twice". By that I mean create a list of every accomplishment you can think of. Don't limit it to work-related situations.

Include travel experiences, educational achievements, volunteer work and leadership opportunities.

- Create a paper file to remind yourself of how great you are. Include every document you can find to back up your accomplishments. Examples may consist of performance evaluations, work samples, certificates, letters of recommendation, written articles and awards. Use it for interviews, revising your resume, preparing your quarterly update for your boss, etc.
- Write out some concise statements about situations where you took action and achieved positive results. Companies love things that save money, manpower and time, as well as bring in new customers and increase profits in any way.

Use your self-marketing scripts anytime you are talking to others about work — during lunch, at the gym, at volunteer committee meetings or professional association meetings.

## Ask for "Out of the Box" Assignments

Have you noticed that most people develop selective hearing when asked to run a company-wide charity campaign, organize the company outing or write the newsletter? This is where you step in. Volunteer for things that others avoid like the plague. We all have skills that we want to promote that are not a part of our current position requirements. The best way to do that is to just step up to the plate and go for it!

## Make Sure People Know Who You Are

Working on company-wide projects allows you to know people from different departmental silos, as well as the opportunities, practices and challenges in each of these areas. Use this newly found information to sniff out valued skills and traits. Start developing these skills yourself!

## Be Consistent in the Image You Present to the World

Make it your standard to "do what you say you are going to do", and you will build a reputation of a person who follows through and can be counted on. Communicate your value in every single action. For example:

- send e-mails without errors
- be professional and energetic every time you answer the phone
- dress well every day
- keep your hair neatly styled
- make it a point to provide at least one small, but meaningful contribution in every meeting

Power is perception. When you think confidently, you will be perceived as confident and will naturally rise to the top.

## Select an Industry Mentor

While it is important to nurture relationships *inside* your company, you also want to build a team of supporters *outside* of your organization. After establishing a rapport with someone you admire, ask them to become your mentor. Let them know exactly how you best learn. Keep them posted on your goals and accomplishments and how they can support you. An across-industry network builds your support infrastructure. Remember — you will only be at your current job an average of three years, so keep planning for the future.

The biggest key to self-promotion is to be consistent in your actions and bold about asking others for assistance.

Figure out exactly where you are headed. When you know precisely where that is, start talking about it to everyone who will listen. The odds are in your favor that they might have some directions and shortcuts for getting there!

# CHAPTER TEN

---

# *Leading the Pack –*
# *Management Success Skills*

# Management—Your Ticket to Career Happiness?

*"People can be divided into three groups: those who make things happen, those who watch things happen, and those who wonder what happened."*

*— John Newber*

$M$anagement—the benchmark of success in anyone's career. Or is it? For those who fall in the era of the baby boomer or earlier, the idea was to work your way up the career ladder. Achieving a management position signified success and power. In my role as a career coach, I've encountered increasingly high numbers of people in the past five years who have achieved success in their roles in management and are more than ready to give it up. They've had enough of the leadership role and are relinquishing their "power" roles for more personal career satisfaction.

Why is this happening? One reason is that management was once a role that signified status, higher responsibility levels, more decision making power, and yes, more money! When the era of downsizing began, the manager's role suddenly included giving the news to valued employees (who they had often personally recruited) that there was no longer a place for them in the company. The Dilbert syndrome was just a little bit TOO real!

## What Does it Take to be a Leader?

If your career goal includes working your way into a leadership role, take time to examine your motivations. While countless competencies are required to be an accomplished leader, check out these basic ideas. You may save yourself valuable time and energy in your decision making process.

- Ability to Lead by Example. Some leaders see their role as delegator and supreme ruler. In reality, a manager is closely observed by all and it's hard to hide flaws. Your own work ethic must be impeccable and epitomize integrity. The tone and example of the work environment comes from the top down. This means that if you spend your time cutting out early, showing up late, relying on all of your outdated skills and complaining about whatever, the people who report to you will no doubt follow your lead!
- Listen, Listen, Listen! A leader can learn more by just asking relevant questions than any other method. It is imperative that you tune in and heed the information you pick up. While the manager's role is to ultimately give direction, the only way to ensure that the direction is on track is to have a realistic finger on the pulse of activity. Some managers fall short in listening, as they *just know* they have all the answers already! Or they don't *have time* to collaborate. The folks actually doing the work inevitably have terrific ideas from their perspective of things. They deserve a conduit to the top—their manager.
- Revel in the Role of Encourager and Buffer. When things go right, the credit belongs with the team. And

when things go wrong, the blame goes to the manager who is ultimately responsible. At times, it can be tough to take the heat. In the big scheme of things, it will be no secret who is motivating and supporting the team—and that will be your payoff. When mistakes are made, you need to step right up to the plate to fix them, and brainstorm on how to prevent the same situation from occurring in the future. Your team needs you to champion their causes and act as the mouthpiece to voice their concerns.

- **Be Change Hearty.** Resisting change will come naturally to most people in the workplace, so the leader's role is one that must embrace and affect it. Obviously, making changes just to see things done differently is not the way to accomplish your goals. The work environment will grow stagnant and never improve without fresh ideas and techniques. The key is to evaluate and implement whenever possible and skip expending energy on trying to hold back the wave of change. Teaching your team members how to thrive in times of change will build synergy and lead people to self-reliance.
- **Growth Orientation.** Today's employees expect and deserve opportunities to learn and grow. It doesn't take formal learning—it's can be equally effective to consistently assign each employee with tasks that maximize the use of their motivated skills and unique talents. The motivated skills are the ones a person LOVES to use—not just where competencies lie. You'll need to seek out stretch assignments to ensure that your team can learn in a safe environment. When challenge and growth is in the picture, productivity is high and turnover diminishes.
- **Support and Model Career Planning.** When you take the attitude that the new worker must build their own career plan, you will have people knocking

down the doors to work under your direction. Some managers tend to discover a person's strengths and use them to gain their OWN success regardless of what the employee's goal is. The trick is to find out where the employee wants to end up and give each person the tools and assignments they need to get there. They'll end up working very hard for you and will always be employable — a win-win for all involved. After all, if you do someday need to downsize, you won't be putting your talent out on the street unprepared for the world of employment at large.

If the ideas I've covered sound like they are aligned with your own personal style, you are definitely on the path to being a good manager. Lead by example. Actively listen. Encourage and mediate for your team. Be a catalyst for change. Encourage continuous growth and learning. Promote personal career planning. These basics will support building your legacy as a successful manager!

# Market Trends for Middle Management

---

*"When he was younger, we called our huntin'*
*dog 'employee' because he was always*
*enthusiastic and ready to go out under any*
*condition and chase birds. Now we call him*
*'manager' because all he wants to do is sit on his*
*tail, bark and point."*

*— Old Southern Joke*

---

Great news for middle managers! Your skills are in back
in demand. The era of cutting management positions by
the thousands seems to be over — at least for now. For
workers in the 40+ range who felt discarded during the
90's, today's business trends point to a growing need for
leaders with successful track records.

In the business model of decades past, the individuals
with the most seniority were the ones further up the ladder.
They were the ones in charge. For workers in the middle to
last quarter of their careers, their positions may have
required little more than directing others what to do.
Today's business environment often puts individuals with
the most in demand skills or the most money in positions of
power. A critical challenge is to incorporate real leadership

skills with the high tech, high function skills in today's managers.

## Trend for Contract Positions

While it may go against the grain for many management level professionals, contract assignments are on the rise. A company's demand for a specific skill set for a finite amount of time is higher than ever. In manufacturing, as business became more sophisticated, the "just in time" (JIT) process was instituted. JIT parts were ordered, JIT inventory levels maintained, JIT orders were produced and shipped JIT to customers. This method ensured less capital tied up in supplies and fewer excess parts, products and so on. Now, there is a growing need for JIT *management*.

Let's say a merger or acquisition has taken place. A team of managers is needed for a limited period of time to perform due diligence, appraise assets and redundancies. They then need to develop and recommend a strategic plan. In numerous instances, this type of skill is not readily available in house. Or perhaps, the internal players are biased in their thinking and recommendations as their own positions may ultimately be at stake.

Mid-level managers need to consider changing their mental programming regarding contract or temporary assignments. This type of work is not just for manual day laborers in today's business world. Some may tend to worry about benefits and "job security" In reality, security stems from the ability to be marketable at *any* stage of a career. When skills are kept up to date and a marketing mentality is embraced, employment possibilities are endless.

## Strategic Management Opportunities

The dot.com phenomenon surprised many Wall Street forecasters and made a tremendous positive financial impact on the economy. Problem was, very few ultimately reached the IPO level. The cycle from start-up to taking a business to the next level is one of the toughest and the juncture where many go under.

Several years ago, there was such a glut of MBA holders that the credential wasn't as valued as it was decades ago. Several firms I consulted with even stated that they weren't interested in MBA candidates, as their thinking was "too textbook" and commonplace—they were looking for individuals who operated more out of the box. Now, the demand for MBAs with strategic business development knowledge is rising at a quickening pace.

While there are some incredibly bright young people who have created and nurtured scores of start-up businesses, these firms are now actively recruiting more seasoned business professionals to lead them to the next level. Their tactical knowledge often just isn't enough to grow the company past the initial phases. This is a perfect spot for middle managers to step in and apply their proven skills.

## Freelance Consulting

The growth of the consulting industry continues to rise because of the critical need for outside advisors. Subject area experts can bring a whole new perspective in evaluating business operations. While there is a plethora of people out there calling themselves "experts", the true consultant is invaluable to any business and provides a global view by applying best practices. Mid-level managers are the prime source to act as the proven experts.

One key advantage to utilizing the services of a consultant is that their perspective is entirely different than that of someone involved from the inside of a firm. First of all, they do not bring an emotionally biased viewpoint when making critical decisions.

A project I consulted on involved the potential

outsourcing of key areas of a large organization. The research, findings, and subsequent recommendations were based on many factors—including the impact on morale and productivity the outsourcing would no doubt have on other divisions. The findings overwhelmingly supported the outsourcing—a move strongly opposed by internal players. When the overall picture was presented, insiders agreed that not only was it the right move, it was one they would not have made without outside counsel.

## Back by Popular Demand

While the ever-growing need for skilled professionals rises with the war for talent, the population of working aged adults continues to shrink. The Baby Boomers are turning 50 at the rate of 11,000 per day and many are thinking retirement. The trend toward portfolio careers and never really "retiring" dovetails perfectly with this statistic. Middle Managers are back in demand . . . and more marketable than ever!

# Jump-start Your Influence as a Manager

---

*"Never tell people how to do things.*
*Tell the what to do and they will surprise you*
*with their ingenuity."*

*— George S. Patton*

---

You've just been promoted or accepted a management position with a new firm. You're enthusiastic and ready to step up to the challenge, but you don't quite know where to start. Here's your 8 Step Plan for getting off to a shining start!

## Meet with Your Manager

Get off on the right foot with an organizational meeting. Many firms, when bringing in new employees/managers, simply show them to their cubicles and leave them on their own.

If this happens to you, try these strategies for turning the tide:

- Request a meeting with your manager to determine exactly what he/she expects you to accomplish during the first 30 days.

- Make a list of projects with top priority.
- Find out exactly how your performance will be evaluated over the next six months.
- Begin submitting a list of your key accomplishments and goals on a weekly basis.

## Find Out How Things Get Done

Take time up-front to closely observe the culture and how work gets done. What is the political system? Most of us say we "hate office politics", but politics are simply the way people communicate — and it is important. Who are the key players? Build some relationships across departments and observe how the company works together as a whole.

## Get to Know Your Staff

Spend lots of time with your new staff, no matter how busy you are or how many voice mails you have to answer. Take time to:

- Walk around and engage in brief interactions with staff members.
- Observe who surfaces as a leader, gets work done quickly and is great at follow-up.
- Meet with your staff each morning for 20 minutes as a routine communication vehicle to establish daily goals and team-building exercises.
- Meet with each staff member individually to discover their preferred skills, work habits, career goals and motivators.

## Pay Attention and Take Notes

As you learn your way around the organization, make sure you really pay attention to your experiences and observations. Create a notebook of ideas and jot down names of people you think would benefit and/or support you in implementing them. Find out what has been tried in the past — and why things may have failed. Keep your ideas to yourself, however, for at least the first several weeks. Making quick changes will most likely create problems down the road.

## Observe and Document

During the first two to four weeks, when you are observing and building, keep in close touch with your manager. Make sure you are over-communicating about progress, tasks and expectations. If open, honest communication is the norm from the onset, your business relationship will prosper. Many of us rely too much on our "intuition" to figure out what someone expects. Ask, and you will always be right on target.

## Organize the Work

Now that you have a feel for your staff, their strengths, weaknesses and preferences, start delegating. Assign projects that are short-term and will quickly build success for everyone on the team. If you make time up-front to assign people duties they truly enjoy carrying out, they will go beyond your wildest expectations in terms of performance.

## Standardize Communication

Set up standard ways of communicating and stick to them. When managing staff, I make it a practice of writing personal notes, cards and e-mails, and leaving voice mails to each person recognizing them for their accomplishments. Daily work group meetings give each person a means of expressing a need for help, informing the group of goals, etc.

## Create Your "Love Me" File

Most of us have been programmed not to "toot our own horns" or brag. The brutal truth is that those who most effectively promote their skills and accomplishments are the ones who get the most rewarding assignments. Keep a file with copies of all kudos letters, course completion certificates, project statistics, and so on. When it is time for your first review, you will be prepared with details of all of your achievements.

The most successful managers are the ones who truly tune in to their staff and take time to discover what motivates each individual. Giving stretch assignments in a safe environment will be something you are remembered for . . . along with your reputation for running a terrific team!

# Managing Different
# Employee Types

---

*"Each man has his own vocation; his talent is
his call. There is one direction where all space
is open to him."*

*— Ralph Waldo Emerson*

---

$A$ Manager wears many masks. Mentor. Delegate.
Motivator. Disciplinarian. Strategist. Team CFO. While I
have met many competent managers in my business
wanderings, I rarely meet one who truly takes time to tune
in to each team member and directly appeal to that
individual's communication style. And the ones that do are
extraordinarily successful.

> *'There's nothing so unequal as the
> equal treatment of unequals.
> "Individualize your leadership."*
>
> *— Unknown*

Think back to the last meeting you attended. More than
likely, there were different personality types represented. A
skillful manager takes these differences and capitalizes on

them to create a high-performing team. Does that sound like the outcome of your meeting?

Why all the gung-ho, rah-rah "high performing team" focus? One word: *profitability*. The biggest differentiater between organizations is human capital. People who find energizing, growth-oriented work environments generally stay longer. And they add more value while they are there. So, if we accept the fact that workers typically change jobs every two to five years, it becomes clear why skilled managers are in demand.

## The I-Speak® Process

Drake Beam Morin developed a widely used assessment tool based upon the work of Dr. Carl Jung, renowned Swiss psychologist: I-Speak Your Language®. The instrument has applications for both business and personal situations and can be quite easily interpreted. Tuning in to others' styles allows us to adapt our approach. The result is that we connect and build honest rapport much more quickly.

There are four basic styles of communication outlined in DBM's tool: Feeling, Sensing, Thinking, and Intuitive.

## The Feeler Style

This style has a time orientation relating to the past and places a high value on how situations impact people. Feelers are typically loyal, persuasive and traditional. They enjoy interaction with other team members, are empathetic and quite skilled at "reading between the lines".

## Management Strategy:

Feelers are quite tuned into the emotions and reactions of others. Let them know how you *feel* about their performance. Find commonalties such as recreational activities or family. Ask them about their take on the synergy of the team and how it could be improved. Express that their ability to interact so well with others is an asset to the team. Make time to chat on a regular basis and follow up with emails and voice mails about their performance as well.

## The Senser Style

Sensers value implementation and action. They are the drivers who have the skill to translate plans into profits. They are successful at getting projects off the ground and covering all the bases. Sensers typically operate in the present time frame, are status seekers and tend toward perfectionism.

## Management Strategy:

The Senser will feel most comfortable when you avoid going into too much detail, and keep your conversations mostly work related. Assign tasks that require them to getting things rolling NOW. Ask for brief status reports and leave voice and emails rather than tracking them down to talk face to face. Give deadlines to adhere to and expect multi-tasking. Don't let this team member get bored—they will stray in a heartbeat if their work environment feels stagnant.

## The Intuitor Style

The visionary is skilled at long range planning and creating original ideas. They are able to forecast trends and tend to value ideas, future thinking and innovation. This employee is able to come up with resourceful ways to approach old problems and can breathe new life into slumping projects.

# Management Strategy

Reach the Intuitors on your team by challenging them to come up with new applications for product or services. Provide an environment that recognizes and rewards ideas resulting in profit. Afford them the autonomy to create, and remember that they may be a little on the unrealistic side. Give them the resources to put real numbers to their ideas to determine feasibility.

# The Thinker Style

The Thinker places high value on statistics, logic and precise procedures. They are objective and excel at analyzing. This employee is challenged when given the opportunity to audit projects, check out all the details and find ways to maximize profits. A Thinker may be over-cautious, and they have the ability to see the impact of the past, present and future when weighing risks. This means they rarely overlook important details.

# Management Strategy

Thinkers go strictly by the book when they approach situations, so try to do the same when dealing with them. Provide plenty of time to discuss objectives in a calm, factual, systematic manner. Get a Thinker's attention by supporting your ideas with facts. Look for things that may go wrong and let them come up with options in advance. Get them involved in creating and documenting step-by-step procedures.

# The Manager Sets the Tone for Communication

A leader who values human capital can easily create a work environment supporting open interchange and capitalizing on differences. Each style of communicating shows advantages and weaknesses. It's your job as leader to seek out and then meet the individual needs of each team member. Emphasize strengths by taking time to observe and tune in and your team will outperform all the others.

# Are You A Micromanager?

*"Nothing is impossible for the man who doesn't have to do it* himself."

*— A.H. Weiler*

Of all the dreaded management styles to work for, the micromanager is right up there at the top of the list along with the bully and the boss who steals your ideas. If you have worked with a micromanager, you KNOW exactly what I mean, and probably would do just about anything to avoid repeating the experience. If you ARE one, you probably don't even recognize it . . . so read on and ask if any of these points sounds familiar.

## Micromanagement Behaviors

- ✓ You tell your staff *exactly* how to do things.
- ✓ You don't have the technical skills your staff members do, but you *still* insist on telling them precisely how to get things done.
- ✓ You have the need to be involved in *everything* and constantly check in to see how things are going.
- ✓ You require that your staff is accountable to you for even minute details.

✓ You don't trust staff members to make and/or implement decisions—after all it is YOU who are ultimately accountable.

✓ You chart out virtually every move to be made in getting the job done.

✓ You track status of progress to the nth degree and know exactly how much time will be needed to complete a task.

If you see yourself in *even one* of these points, you are probably in danger of being labeled as a micromanager—a severely career-limiting label to earn.

## Did Command and Control EVER work?

The management style of the early 20th century was quite often based on the labor of unskilled workers. Workers typically performed one function and really didn't have a grasp on the big picture. In this environment, the leader was the individual responsible for pulling all of the pieces together.

During this time, micromanagement was actually needed to keep machines running, get products produced on time and to keep workers on task. Without the direction of the "boss man", workers literally didn't know how to proceed. Few workers had any decision making power and were monitored by a time clock for everything from work hours to breaks. Companies viewed workers as people from whom they "bought time". And micromanaging them was the only means to ensure that production quotas were met.

## From Unskilled to Skilled Workers

Over time, businesses became more and more complicated and the emphasis shifted to productivity. In the 1980's, Total

Quality Management and process reengineering entered the picture. At this point, the focus shifted to more complicated procedures which also required employees to become more skilled. The more skilled workers were, the more valuable they became to the company. People began to learn that they could change companies if they were unhappy with their position or felt they weren't treated well.

Today, we have evolved into a highly complex business world driven by results, profits and competition. Workers are known as team member or partners. Skills are built through experience and continuous learning. Team members generally stay at a firm from two to five years and when they leave, they take their skills and experience with them. This means that the company loses these assets and has to constantly rebuild.

## Shortage of Skilled Workers

When a manager looks at his human resources as expendable, trouble starts. The Talent War currently raging means that there are just not enough skilled workers to meet the demand. With 11,000 Baby Boomers a day turning 50, the workforce is quickly shrinking. This all points to the reason micromanagers are no longer effective. People are hired for their talent . . . and in many cases ironically, the less experienced workers are frequently the most highly skilled. This means that managers are often delegating to staff members younger and yet more skilled than themselves.

## Why do People Leave?

The top reason employees leave a company is that they do not feel appreciated. Managers are the ones who hold the key to building and retaining the human capital of the firm.

Studies show that people will stay in a company for less money and even for less responsibility — IF they are working for a manager who creates an environment that provides a positive culture, autonomy and consistent learning opportunities.

## The Modern Manager's Mission

Today's manager is the direct opposite of the micromanager described above. She views associates as assets who need to be valued and protected. Assets that will perform to top capability when they know they are valued.

A manager's prime mission is to ensure that the associates have every tool and resource needed to carry out their job function. In today's highly skilled workplace, a manager often has little or no personal knowledge of how to perform the tasks their staff carries out on a daily basis. The sooner they accept that they need to keep their ego in their back pocket and focus on what the team needs, the quicker they will see productivity rise and turnover decrease.

# Power Coaching

"New frames of reference touch people with
new possibilities and choices and
lead to new skills and capabilities."

— Robert Hargrove

The role of the leader has evolved from absolute ruler to coach and supporter. Today's manager is there to ensure that team members have every tool and skill they need to succeed. It was much easier to "manage" under the former business model, where the top management level decided what needed to be done and middle managers directed the worker bees. The usefulness of this hierarchical model has long since dissolved. Now, a manager's focus should be forming a collaborative relationship with each member of his or her staff.

## What Coaching Isn't

Coaching isn't providing analysis, therapy or counseling. And it's not trying to figure out where a person came from or why they think the way they do. It also isn't focusing on an individual's weaknesses or finding ways to "fix" them. Not everyone is a "star", and an astute manager will support each person in being all they want to be.

# What Coaching Is

A coach meets an individual exactly where they are at that moment. Always a few steps ahead, a coach observes, collaborates and finds ways to support staff members in their development. Acting as the student's "headlights", the coach shows him/her ways to push forward.

# Why Coach?

When an organization provides direction and support, along with appropriate training, each employee has the opportunity to rise to excellence, rather than be limited in one role. This growth means enhanced creativity and higher productivity. Teams flourish, turnover decreases, goals are met and everybody wins.

Coaching is a terrific means of helping someone take his or her desires to the highest level. Problems can be eliminated early when employees are provided with a nonjudgmental resource for sharing information.

# Setting the Tone

A manager's coaching style is dependent upon personality, work environment, gender—the list goes on. An effective coach needs to display the ability to observe without judging and treat each encounter with absolute confidentiality. Frustrated team members must have permission to vent without consequences, express opinions and show vulnerabilities.

It's paramount for a coach to possess highly developed communication skills and be willing to be "real". A few nicks and bruises here and there make our journeys more interesting. The coach must be committed to honesty and uncovering lessons gradually as they occur—like peeling an onion. As the student is ready to learn, the coach's job is to provide unlimited, relevant "field work" allowing the person to gradually evolve and learn when a topic is relevant.

The role of coach also requires being down in the trenches with the team, as well as available and generous with time. As a corporate change consultant, I frequently work with teams in transition and hear "manager" horror stories, such as "My boss puts a sign on her door at least three days a week, declaring 'Bad Mood—Go Away.'"

## Giving Feedback

At the beginning of the coaching relationship, the parties set out by identifying key goals. Performance expectations are outlined and discussed in detail. Next, the parties set a schedule and means of regular communication about issues, questions and concerns. It just doesn't cut it to pass someone in the hall and ask, "How's it going?"

In my experience, a weekly communication showing accomplishments, overall challenges and goals for the coming week provides the fastest opportunity for growth. It sets accountability, expectations and motivates action.

## Be Direct

The word "feedback" often carries a negative connotation. Instead, use it as a means of giving valuable information to your team members. Positive feedback is terrific when several others are around. And be specific in noting the exact behaviors you observe. The pat phrase "nice job" is more meaningful when specifics are stated. For example, you can try:

> *"Julie, I was impressed with the skillful way you communicated with that irate client. He definitely went away feeling like he had been listened to and*

*his problem was solved. It's terrific to have your talent on our team!"*

Give feedback in areas that the team member can control. If they can't do anything about it, it starts a back-and-forth exchange that goes nowhere. Come up with creative ways to address the issues and move forward.

## Partner—Don't Solve!

The key to successful coaching is to never give the employee the solution to a situation—learning comes from deciding the direction and action to take.

Providing continuous safety nets will ensure the job will get done without compromising time.

The most fulfilling task for a manager is being an honest, open, supportive sounding board to a colleague. Remember to be a coach—not a therapist, mentor or friend. Be a master facilitator of positive actions!

# Building High-Performance Teams

*"Teamwork is so important that it is virtually impossible for you to reach the heights of your capabilities or make the money that you want without becoming very good at it."*

*— Brian Tracy*

The increased value of working in teams is touted by many as the key change in business during the 90s. In my work with corporate clients, I often hear that they desire to work in a team that is *"really a team"*. It seems that teams often divide work without actually improving the group's performance.

Groups are the most natural forms for interaction at work. We are innately pack animals — ever since caveman times, when humans lived in herds, hunted together and protected one another. And yet, we are not really *good* at teamwork. What separates a *group* from a *high-performance team*?

## The Group Mind Advantage

Hundreds of tests have been conducted to measure the "Group Thinking" advantage. They indicate that 97% of the time, a group achieves higher scores on tests than the individual scores of the best group members. It stands to reason that intelligence should multiply in diverse groups and provide a much better outcome. When all team members are committed, the overall advantages are impressive. A synergy develops, which moves the pace faster, increases communication and ownership, and results in positive outcomes.

## Leadership from the Top Down

Way too many team leaders are ego-driven, not outcome driven. While trying to get the most out of their team, these folks cannot bear the thought of turning the applause over to the team. They want to bask in the glow of the spotlight *themselves.*

Of course, evolved leaders know that they will reap much more attention if they lead their teams to success. Ultimately, the attention does go to the leader — but individual accomplishments go to the team. According to the Center for Creative Leadership, team management skills are the most sought-after managerial competency.

## The Strong Kick-off

When a team is assembled, the first order of business is to set up a meeting with lots of time for brainstorming. During this time, the group sketches out the mission, vision, values and goals of the project. Naturally, these are aligned with the company goals, but the process of the group sketching out their own version is key. Each associate must buy in to the common mission and thoroughly understand how their own work is critical to reaching the goals.

The group combines notes, ideas, debates and humor to create lists of ideas. When completed, one or two members of the team should put the information together and bring it back to the group for final approval. Upon reaching consensus, print the group's information and make it highly visible (on memos, fax cover sheets, posted in common work areas, etc.).

## Role of the Leader

The manager is responsible for setting the tone for the entire group and motivating each member to excellence. Motivation makes all the difference. The behavior and communication style the manager models will be the strongest influence on the team.

Loyalty to a company is no longer high on the list of career management/motivation techniques; however, inspiring loyalty to a manager is very achievable and beneficial. Lead and coach your team, becoming their advocate whenever possible. Make sure that working under your direction is *fun* and provides plenty of growth opportunities.

## Interview Your Crew

When you spend time with each staff member individually, you learn what motivates him or her. Is it recognition? Responsibility? Time off? Technical challenge? Once you know that, you can use the right type of motivation whenever possible.

Interview each person, asking them to describe their key skills. Find out what gets them charged up. When a leader provides each team member the opportunity to stretch and develop new skills, their employees will be motivated to perform. Once you are familiar with their strengths, shamelessly flaunt their skills and give them all the credit when things turn out great.

Above all, to successfully lead a high-performance team, remember to put your ego in your back pocket and leave it there. Make the team members the stars, and they will walk across hot coals for you. Start each day with a quick, 20-minute meeting to set priorities, focus and get everyone running in the same direction. The results will amaze you!

# Motivating Your Employees
# to Peak Performance

---

*"Ability is what you're capable of doing.
Motivation determines what you do. Attitude
determines how well you do it."*

— Lou Holtz

---

The competition is on between organizations to attract the best talent, and in a tight labor market an even tougher challenge is created. While compensation always plays a key role, the intangibles are just as important. An organization's leadership, culture, reputation and morale are also part of the mix. In fact, the relationship between individual contributors and their managers is where it all begins.

Motivating the work force requires building and maintaining a continuous thread as individuals rotate in and out of the organization. Blending the talents of long-term, temporary and consulting employees to reach critical goals requires the glue of *esprit de corps*. The relationship between individual contributors and their managers is crucial to building and maintaining morale, and the concept that morale develops from the top down has been proven in numerous studies. Knowing that a firm needs a common vision is one thing; implementing a motivational strategy is quite another.

In my management experience, I have learned that the easy part is getting the right people in the position — growing and retaining them is where the real skill comes in. I spent four years on the road managing large corporate reorganization projects. My role was to set up a facility, staff it, get programs rolling and act as liaison between the service and client companies. This meant that I often found myself in a strange city, with no resource ideas, and a very short lead time in which to launch a project. Through trial and error, I discovered methods to effectively connect with teams and have come to realize that the small things are what make a **big** difference.

**Let them know your hot buttons.** At each project's kick-off, I held an informal meeting. Those who worked with me on many projects knew that it was time for the "You're either on the team or off the team" speech. Essentially, I set the standard for excellence, letting them know there was to be no compromise. We had a service to deliver to employees who were in transition that would seriously impact their lives in either a positive or negative way. It was our job to ensure that it was positive and that the participants emerged from the situation stronger and smarter.

If staff members could not summon the energy to look enthusiastic for eight hours a day and approach their work as fun, then a transition project was not the right place for them. Somehow, this created a synergetic atmosphere. Some of them often remarked, "This is the first project I have ever worked on where 'fun' was mandated!"

**Ask staff to talk with you about *their* needs and hot buttons.** Hold regular focus group sessions. Hire an outside facilitator to create an open forum for discussing ideas, problems, successes and goals. Set up a vehicle for receiving suggestions from employees in advance to create the agenda. Begin the sessions with time for green-light thinking. Just let the comments and ideas flow. Chart them up. Then use the input to come up with suggestions for activities, change and rewards. Listen! And then follow up with actions responding to each item. Document it all so when an employee asks, "Whatever happened to our idea about . . . ?" there will be a historical log for reference.

**Model the behavior you want to see from your employees.** A manager's role has a huge impact on the attitude of the entire crew. Be open and supportive, providing plenty of opportunities to praise their behavior. Make time to visit with them individually. Tune in. What do they need to get their job done today? How can you support them in reaching their own personal goals? What challenges are they having where your coaching would help out? Communicate high personal values both formally and through day-to-day contact. Smile!

**Personally thank employees when their contribution merits it.** The competitive nature of business can diminish the occasions for praising people. Be an encourager! Build an Applause Wall in an area where there is a lot of traffic, such as around the copier. Post notes, letters, memos, photos — you name it. It will keep the group abreast of what is going on with the team at large, setting an atmosphere of community and support. It will reinforce all that is going right! Invite associates to have a cup of coffee one-on-one to talk about what a difference having them on your team makes. Write short notes — by hand — expressing your appreciation. Or buy a funny card that you know will appeal to their particular sense of humor. Circulate e-mails recognizing positive contributions.

**Expect the most from staff members and they will live up to it.** In short, simply focus on creating an atmosphere of encouragement, growth, play, professionalism, support and optimism. Your team members will do anything to be a part of projects where they come out smarter than they were when they started.

**Grow your employees.** Find out their aspirations. Then provide endless stretch assignments and ensure they have the training they need to reach their goals. Sit down with employees to find out their ultimate goals. Brainstorm ways to grow roots supporting those goals (through professional organizations, community activities or opportunities within the organization). Suggest classes and schedule time for them to attend.

**Reinforce the significance of their diversity.** In the lobby of the Gap's Ontario Distribution Center, there is a large map where each employee has placed a pushpin indicating their birth country. The 64 associates represent 15 countries of origin. The result is a motivating visual display celebrating diversity through heritage. By building an organization that celebrates differences, the outcome will be stronger than you can imagine.

This saying by Lao-tse explains it best: "Go to the people. Learn from them. Love them. Start with what they know. Build on what they have. With the best of leaders, when their task is accomplished, their work is done, the people will remark: We have done it ourselves."

# Landing Venture Capital—
# Hot Executive Skill

---

*"Money is like a sixth sense without
which you cannot make a complete
use of the other five."*

*— W. Somerset Maugham*

---

The money game has always been one of the most intoxicating and addicting games around. Learning how to play and how to hold onto the winnings is one of the most sought after skills for anyone interested in business. The money game and the seemingly unlimited availability of venture capital has been a key factor in the building of the new economy these past few years.

Even through the tide is now turning, and raising capital is still a highly sought-after executive skill. Over the past five or so years we have seen sometimes outrageous funding of IPOs and an incredibly rapid formation of new businesses largely due to developing technology. Some maintain that the days of easy money are quickly coming to an end.

## Profitability is King

Many of the dot.coms formed supported the dreams and

ideas of incredibly talented individuals. The fact is, there was little to substantiate the rate of growth of ventures and the real market for new products. In some cases, the products were there, but the ability to deliver was lacking. In other cases, it was difficult to even find a real product.

In countless cases, venture capital was raised on projections unsubstantiated by anything other than enthusiasm and genius. The phenomenon of presenting a business plan and getting instantly financed is rapidly changing to the requirement of presenting a real business plan. Building bona fide financial models substantiating the point where profits can realistically be expected is taking the place of presenting "too good to be true" ideas.

## Frugality is the Buzz Word

We all remember the millions spent on advertising and branding during the millennium. The 2000 Super Bowl was watched by many just to view the dot.com ads reign and marvel over the millions invested in these one shot advertising plans. The days of $10 million budgets spent on Olympics or Super Bowl ads is most likely behind the majority of start-up companies. The trend is shifting back to airing more on the conservative side until a revenue stream is in place. Building bridges between venture capital, reaching the initial public offering stage and earning loyal customers is the answer to this shift.

Pitching ideas to venture capitalists and landing funding is a skill that has become increasingly difficult. The task of courting and winning over investors now requires the answering of skeptical questions, presentation of business models, endless data and rigorous demands.

## Faster Burn Rates

A Catch-22 in the process of taking a business from initial

start-up and product development is the need for increasing numbers of people. And of course this means a need for increasing amounts of money to pay those people. New companies can operate on a shoestring with very limited physical space and typically, few luxuries and little inventory. As the headcount rises, more spending is required and the "burn rate" — the rate at which the money is spent — rises right along with it. With more headcount, government regulations can play a bigger role, which also muddies the water.

## Higher Stakes

Investment monies are always going to be available, but the "price" goes up as the demand rises. When a firm invests, a representative looking out for their interests earns a place on the start-up's Board of Directors. This means less flexibility in operating and quick decision making.

The term "significant liquidation preferences" is one that can put a damper on a creative and enthusiastic entrepreneur's fire. The term means that if progress doesn't meet the expectations of the investors, they can literally demand the right to force the sale of the company to free up their cash and let them out of their investment.

## Money Attracting Strategies

For executives focusing their attention on raising capital for startups, learning by the success of others is the best way to gain a lead on the rest of the pack. A few strategies that have worked well in attracting financing include:

- Product Viability. The product has to be without a doubt, heads above the competition. A worldwide market possible through the web is a must — and the industry must show huge growth potential. And above all, it must be a product that brings real change to the industry it is entering—not just another good idea.

- Management Team. The clincher is having a management team in place that can take the product to the highest level. Enthusiasm, bright ideas and dreams are appreciated, but flexibility and cross-functional skills are mandatory. The team must have solid experience in technology, operations and finance and be able to adjust at the drop of a hat.
- Multiple Sources of Revenue. Considering the volatility of the market and an economy that fluctuates rapidly, a business sustained by multiple streams of revenue is highly attractive. A strong customer base coupled with the forecast of high margins will allow a fledgling business to stay afloat through multiple changes.

When it comes to capital and the role executives play in locating not only numerous, but the RIGHT sources, the game is become exceedingly competitive. The ability to consistently make smart choices in locating capital and negotiate the best terms will earn an executive a place at the top.

# Building A Creative
# Work Environment

---

*"The chief enemy of creativity is*
*"good" sense."*

*— Pablo Picasso*

---

$A$s the world moves faster and faster, organizations strain to gain a competitive edge. One of the deciding factors for success is the ability to build and continuously motivate creative thinking in the work force. Only by consistently reinventing our products, services and processes can we stay at the head of the pack.

In the past, creativity hasn't been one of the more tangibly marketable skills in general business. Companies often rewarded hard skills, such as those involving computers, finance and science. Now even highly technical professionals need to be creative to be involved in the top projects. It is the responsibility of each and every organization to build an environment that encourages and rewards creativity.

## A Creative Physical Environment

The starting point for a creative work force is a positive physical work environment — lots of windows, soothing colors in individual work areas and energizing colors in communal areas. One firm with which I consulted used brightly colored pipes in open ceilings to divide team/ departmental areas from large pods, with movable walls for team meetings. The result was that coaching, feedback, collaboration and communication reached an all-time high. When working side-by-side, employees learned to use their unique strengths, bouncing ideas off one another as part of their routine process.

## Minimize Bureaucracy

An atmosphere of openness and creativity has to start at the top and trickle down. This is one of the few areas that will not grow with a grassroots initiative. By providing both management and staff with the same basic work environment, barriers are literally removed. If managers make it a habit to practice MBWA (Management By Walking Around), they will build a more open level of communication and have plenty of face time with staff. Maintaining communication with each and every employee allows management to see, hear, feel and touch problems and challenges.

## Hire Opposites

My work in career management has brought me into contact with scores of hiring managers. One thing they agree on is that when it comes right down to the final decision, if two candidates are equal on paper and interview equally well, they hire the one they like the most — the one they want to spend a third or more of their life with. This is the first place to let go of what is comfortable and achieve breakthrough creativity by hiring opposites.

To truly function as a creative team, the mix of skills and traits needs to transcend the EEO Regulations covering race, creed or sexual preference, and embrace *all* differences — in years of experience, expertise in other industries, countries and size of companies. Differences in age, education level and personality type bring perspectives you would never achieve with a homogeneous work team.

## Collaborative Meetings

Creativity is not something that can be turned on and off. Meetings offer a collaborative effort, where every employee can contribute new ideas and different ways of thinking, as well as have fun and take risks. Instead of a meeting being one of the most dreaded times at work, it can be thought of as something positive. A strong support network within the company is necessary — one that encourages each person as an individual contributor without judging the feasibility of ideas.

Arrange the meeting room so that every participant can see one another, such as in a square formation. Next, provide toys. Markers and paper, Play-Doh®, Slinkys® and stress balls encourage participants to let their guard down and get physically involved. This naturally leads to more mental stimulation and a smoother path to creativity.

## Keep it Simple

When working on collaborative efforts, break down goals and tasks into components. The simpler each component of the project is, the more open and creative we become. I love the story of the man who lodged his tractor-trailer in an underpass after discovering too late that his load was too high. Police and emergency crews used fire trucks and heavy equipment to try pulling the semi first forward, then backward, through the underpass. Finally, a little boy passed by and said . . . "Why don't you just let the air out of the tires of the truck . . . it will be lower and the truck will fit under the bridge." It took the creative mind of a little boy to solve the problem dozens of "experienced professionals" couldn't solve.

## Reward Creativity

Most employees would rather love their work, be told they are doing a great job and receive positive reinforcement and recognition than get a raise. If a new idea is proposed by an employee and then implemented, by all means, share the reward with the employee—both financially and with company recognition.

Write up success stories about ideas that made a difference and place them in the company newsletter or intranet. Reward the employee with time off, extra perks or even a reserved parking spot in a choice location.

Begin infusing your organization with creative juices today. It will help employees cope with change, inspire teamwork, enhance communication, and boost productivity and morale.